Photo by T. Charles Erickson
A scene from the Broadway production of "Swinging on a Star." Set design by Jim Youmans.

SWINGING ON A STAR

(The Johnny Burke Musical)

Lyrics by
JOHNNY BURKE

Music by
JOHNNY BURKE, JOE BUSHKIN,
ERROLL GARNER, ROBERT HAGGART,
ARTHUR JOHNSTON, JAMES MONACO,
HAROLD SPINA, JIMMY VAN HEUSEN

Written by
MICHAEL LEEDS

★

★

DRAMATISTS
PLAY SERVICE
INC.

SPECIAL NOTE

Anyone receiving permission to produce SWINGING ON A STAR is required to give the following credits on the title page of all programs distributed in connection with performances of the Play. In all instances in which the title of the Play appears for purposes of advertising, publicizing or otherwise exploiting the Play and/or a production thereof the credit shall read SWINGING ON A STAR The Johnny Burke Musical. The name of Johnny Burke must appear on a separate line, in which no other name appears, immediately beneath the title and in size of type equal to 50% of the largest, most prominent letter used for the title of the Play. No person, firm or entity may receive credit larger or more prominent than that accorded Johnny Burke. On the title page, the names of the Composers, Writer and Broadway Producers must be no less than 35% of the size of the largest, most prominent letter used in the title of the Play:

SWINGING ON A STAR
The Johnny Burke Musical

Lyrics by
Johnny Burke

Music by
Johnny Burke, Joe Bushkin, Erroll Garner, Robert Haggart,
Arthur Johnston, James Monaco, Harold Spina, Jimmy Van Heusen

Written by
Michael Leeds

SWINGING ON A STAR was originally produced on Broadway by
Richard Seader * Mary Burke Kramer * Paul B. Berkowsky
and Angels of the Arts

Originally produced at George Street Playhouse, Gregory S. Hurst, Producing Artistic Director

Additionally produced both in workshop and on the mainstage of the Goodspeed Opera House,
Michael P. Price, Executive Director

SPECIAL NOTE ON SLIDES

The use of the photographic slides and accompanying cassette tapes, as suggested in this Play, is optional and are available through the Play Service.

SWINGING ON A STAR was produced on Broadway by Richard Seader, Mary Burke Kramer, Paul B. Berkowsky and Angels of the Arts, at the Music Box Theater, in New York City on October 6, 1995. It was directed by Michael Leeds; the set design was by Jim Youmans; the costume design was by Judy Dearing; the lighting design was by Richard Nelson; the sound design was by T. Richard Fitzgerald; the choreography was by Kathleen Marshall; the dance music arrangements were by Peter Howard; the musical direction, orchestrations and vocal arrangements were by Barry Levitt; the additional musical arrangements were by Ron Drotos and the production stage manager was Mary Porter Hall. The cast included Terry Burrell, Lewis Cleale, Denise Faye, Kathy Fitzgerald, Eugene Fleming, Alvaleta Guess and Michael McGrath.

CHARACTERS

ACT ONE

SPEAKEASY — Chicago

THE WAITER .... MAN 2
MAME .... WOMAN 3
REGINALD .... MAN 1
CLEO .... WOMAN 2
JEANNIE .... WOMAN 1
FLORA .... WOMAN 4
BEN .... MAN 3

DEPRESSION — The Bowery

THE HOMELESS MAN .... MAN 1
THE STREET PEOPLE .... MAN 3/WOMAN 1/WOMAN 2/WOMAN 3
THE POLISH GENTLEMAN .... MAN 2
THE HOUSEWIFE .... WOMAN 4
THE SUITORS .... MAN 1/MAN 2/MAN 3

RADIO SHOW — New York City

THE HARMONICS .... MAN 3/WOMAN 2/WOMAN 3
THE ANNOUNCER .... MAN 1
BUDDY .... MAN 2
BETTY .... WOMAN 1
VICKY VOYAY .... WOMAN 4

USO SHOW — The Pacific Islands

MC .... MAN 2
BUZZ ALBRIGHT .... MAN 3
MISS SOUTH DAKOTA .... WOMAN 4
MISS NORTH CAROLINA .... WOMAN 1
MISS RHEINGOLD .... WOMAN 3
LENA GEORGE .... WOMAN 2
EDDIE .... MAN 1

ACT TWO

BALLROOM — Hotel Roosevelt, Akron Ohio

THE MANAGER .... MAN 1
THE COAT CHECK GIRL .... WOMAN 1
THE WAITER .... MAN 3
THE VOCALIST .... WOMAN 3
THE MAN .... MAN 2
THE DATE .... WOMAN 4
THE WOMAN ALONE .... WOMAN 2

ROAD TO... — Paramount Studios, Hollywood

BING .... MAN 1
BOB .... MAN 2
DOROTHY .... WOMAN 4
THE SHEIK .... MAN 3
GIRLS .... WOMAN 1/WOMAN 3
SOUTHERN WOMAN .... WOMAN 2

STARLIGHT SUPPER CLUB — Manhattan

THE LOVERS .... MAN 1 & WOMAN 1
MAN 2 & WOMAN 2
MAN 3 & WOMAN 3
WOMAN 4

MUSICAL NUMBERS

ACT ONE

SPEAKEASY:

YOU'RE NOT THE ONLY OYSTER IN THE STEW (Burke/Spina) .... CLEO/JEANNIE/FLORA
CHICAGO STYLE (Burke/Van Heusen) .... BEN/JEANNIE/FLORA/WAITER
AIN'T IT A SHAME ABOUT MAME (Burke/Monaco) .... BEN/MAME
WHAT'S NEW (Burke/Haggart) .... JEANNIE
DOCTOR RHYTHM (Burke/Monaco) .... CLEO/BEN

DEPRESSION:

PENNIES FROM HEAVEN (Burke/Johnston) .... THE HOMELESS MAN
WHEN STANISLAUS GOT MARRIED (Burke/Van Heusen) .... THE POLISH GENTLEMAN/THE STREET PEOPLE
HIS ROCKING HORSE RAN AWAY (Burke/Van Heusen) ..... THE HOUSEWIFE
ANNIE DOESN'T LIVE HERE ANYMORE (Burke/Young/Spina) .... THE SUITORS

RADIO SHOW:

ANNIE DOESN'T LIVE HERE ANYMORE (Burke/Young/Spina) .... BUDDY/BETTY/THE ANNOUNCER/THE HARMONICS
SCATTERBRAIN (Burke/Keene/Bean/Masters) .... BUDDY
ONE, TWO, BUTTON YOUR SHOE (Burke/Johnston) .... BETTY/BUDDY
WHAT DOES IT TAKE TO MAKE YOU TAKE TO ME? (Burke/Van Heusen) .... VICKY VOYAY
IRRESISTIBLE (Burke/Spina) .... THE ANNOUNCER/VICKY/THE HARMONICS
AN APPLE FOR THE TEACHER (Burke/Johnston) .... ALL

USO SHOW:

THANK YOUR LUCKY STARS AND STRIPES (Burke/Van Heusen) .... MC/BUZZ
PERSONALITY (Burke/Van Heusen) ...... MISS SOUTH DAKOTA/MISS NORTH CAROLINA/MISS RHEINGOLD
THERE'S ALWAYS THE BLUES (Burke/Bushkin) .... LENA
POLKA DOTS AND MOONBEAMS (Burke/Van Heusen) .... EDDIE
SWINGING ON A STAR (Burke/Van Heusen) .... ALL
STARS AND STRIPES (REPRISE) .... ALL

ACT TWO

BALLROOM:

DON'T LET THAT MOON GET AWAY (Burke/Monaco) .... THE WAITER

ALL YOU WANT TO DO IS DANCE (Burke/Johnston)/
YOU DANCED WITH DYNAMITE (Burke/Van Heusen) .... THE DATE/ THE MAN

IMAGINATION (Burke/Van Heusen) .... THE VOCALIST/ THE WAITER/THE COAT CHECK GIRL

IT COULD HAPPEN TO YOU (Burke/Van Heusen) .... THE WOMAN ALONE

ROAD TO...:

ROAD TO MOROCCO (Burke/Van Heusen) .... BING/BOB

APALACHICOLA (Burke/Van Heusen) .... BING/BOB/DOROTHY

YOU DON'T HAVE TO KNOW THE LANGUAGE
(Burke/Van Heusen) .... BING/BOB/GIRLS

GOING MY WAY (Burke/Van Heusen) .... BING

SHADOWS ON THE SWANEE (Burke/Young/Spina) .... SOUTHERN WOMAN/ BING/BOB/DOROTHY

PAKISTAN (Burke/Van Heusen) .... SHEIK/DOROTHY/BING/BOB

ROAD TO MOROCCO (REPRISE) (Burke/Van Heusen) .... BING/ BOB/DOROTHY

SUPPER CLUB:

BUT, BEAUTIFUL (Burke/Van Heusen) .... WOMAN 3

LIKE SOMEONE IN LOVE (Burke/Van Heusen) .... WOMAN 1

MOONLIGHT BECOMES YOU (Burke/Van Heusen) .... MAN 1

IF LOVE AIN'T THERE (IT AIN'T THERE) (Burke) .... MAN 2

SUNDAY, MONDAY OR ALWAYS (Burke/Van Heusen) .... WOMAN 2

MISTY (Burke/Garner) .... MAN 3

HERE'S THAT RAINY DAY (Burke/Van Heusen) .... WOMAN 4

PENNIES FROM HEAVEN (REPRISE) .... ALL

SWINGING ON A STAR (REPRISE) .... ALL

SWINGING ON A STAR

ACT ONE

Scene 1

Time: 1925 — Early evening

Place: A Chicago Speakeasy

Once the audience is settled, the band whips into a swinging "PENNIES FROM HEAVEN." The house lights dim and the table lights go on.

The Speakeasy is open for business.

A Waiter appears in a short-waisted, white jacket. He takes drink orders from the audience members sitting at the front tables blanketing the stage.

Mame and Reginald enter from the back of the house. Mame is stunning; she doesn't so much walk as glide. The Waiter greets her familiarly and seats them at a side table on stage.

Cleo, the owner of the Speakeasy, enters from backstage. She passes among the tables, greeting her customers. Pleasurably surprised to see Mame, she motions to the Waiter that their drinks are on the house. As the band finishes, Cleo steps center.

CLEO. Evenin' ladies and gentlemen, and welcome to my humble establishment. Now, for those of you who are here for the first time, and perhaps a little worried about the long arm of the law, let me give you the short of it. If you see a policeman comin' through the front door, well, that's a raid. If you see a policeman comin' through the side door, well, that's a customer. And if you see a policeman comin' from the back, — *("Preening.")* — well, honey, that's a happy man. So, sit back and drink up. Remember folks, this is a private club, dedicated to preserving the anonymity of its clientele. *(To a man in the audience.)* Ain't that right, Senator? *(The band members shade their eyes to peer at the "Senator.")* Now we're gonna open the show with a little ditty whose lyrics were written by a young man who lives right here in Chicago. His name is ... *(To Bandleader.)* Joe, what's that kid's name?

BANDLEADER. Johnny Burke.

CLEO. Oh, yeah, Johnny Burke. I seen him hangin' around backstage and one of the girls told me he's a good boy. Or did she say, "Boy, was he good!"? Let's give it a go, Joe! *(The band begins a bluesy intro. Cleo moves her hips suggestively to the music.)* Umm, got a nice feel to it ... *(Feeling her hips.)* ... The song, too. *(She sings "YOU'RE NOT THE ONLY OYSTER IN THE STEW.")*

YOU'RE NOT THE ONLY OYSTER IN THE STEW,
"Hear what I'm sayin', Senator?"
YOU'RE NOT THE ONLY TEA LEAF IN THE TEA;
"What's your vote on this motion?"
HOWEVER, I'M CONVINCED,
COMPLETELY AND FULLY AND FIRMLY CONVINCED
THAT YOU'RE THE ONLY ONE FOR ME.
"We'll reconvene later."

(Moving on to someone else.)

YOU'RE NOT THE ONLY WRINKLE ON THE PRUNE;
"No, you're not."
YOU'RE NOT THE ONLY APPLE ON THE TREE.
"Mame knows what I'm talkin' about."

MAME. *(Enthusiastically.)* Yeah, girl!! *(Mame catches Reginald's disapproving eye. She immediately reverts back to the "elegant lady.")*

CLEO.

IT'S STILL AND ALL A FACT,
A PERFECTLY LOGICAL, POSITIVE FACT,
THAT YOU'RE THE ONLY ONE FOR ME.

(On to another.)

YOU'RE SO WELL SUPPLIED WITH THE VERY THINGS I SEEK;
YOUR SMILE IS REFRESHING, YOUR KISSES ARE UNIQUE.
WHEN YOU'RE AROUND I'M SUSCEPTIBLE AND WEAK.
I LOVE YOU —

(Quickly to the man's wife.)

— SO TO SPEAK.
THERE'RE SEVEN MILLION PEOPLE IN NEW YORK,

"I've only met the men."

AND FIFTY MILLION FRENCHMEN IN PAREE,

"Chateaubriand!"

AND NOT TO MENTION SUCH

AS ENGLISH AND IRISH, ITALIAN AND DUTCH,

BUT YOU'RE THE ONLY ONE FOR ME.

(Flora and Jeannie strut onstage.) These are my girls. Tell 'em, ladies.

JEANNIE.

YOU'RE NOT THE ONLY OYSTER IN THE STEW.

CLEO. That's Jeannie.

FLORA.

YOU'RE NOT THE ONLY TUNA IN THE SEA.

CLEO. And that there's Flora.

JEANNIE/FLORA.

BUT, HONEY, YOU'RE THE BEST.

BELIEVE ME, IT'S TRUE —

CLEO. *(Aside.)* 'Cause they've had all the rest.

JEANNIE/FLORA.

BUT, YOU'RE THE ONLY ONE FOR ME.

CLEO. Go make friends, girls. *(Jeannie and Flora head out into the house and play with the men.)*

JEANNIE.

YOU'RE NOT THE ONLY BERRY ON THE BUSH.

CLEO. Take it easy on him, Jeannie.

FLORA.

YOU'RE NOT THE ONLY GOLF BALL ON THE TEE.

JEANNIE/FLORA.

HOWEVER, I'M CONVINCED.

— COMPLETELY

— FULLY

(Putting a man's hand on their thigh or breast.)

— *FIRMLY* CONVINCED

THAT YOU'RE THE ONLY ONE FOR ME!

(Jeannie and Flora head back onstage.)

CLEO.

YOU'RE SO DEBONAIR, YOU'RE SO CHARMING AND SO SWEET,

YOUR LIPS ARE TOO TEMPTING, YOUR DIMPLES CAN'T BE BEAT.

YOUR EARS, YOUR EYES, YOUR NOSE, YOUR CHIN.
I EVEN LOVE YOUR FEET!
"Somebody open a window!"
'CAUSE I CAN'T TAKE THE HEAT!

CLEO/JEANNIE/FLORA.
THERE'RE SEVEN MILLION PEOPLE IN NEW YORK,
AND FIFTY MILLION FRENCHMEN IN PAREE,
AND NOT TO MENTION SUCH AS —

JEANNIE.
— ENGLISH

FLORA.
— IRISH

CLEO.
— ITALIAN

CLEO/JEANNIE/FLORA.
— DUTCH!
BUT YOU'RE THE ONLY ONE FOR ME.

CLEO. I'm a one-man woman.

JEANNIE/FLORA.
YOU'RE THE ONLY ONE FOR ME.

CLEO. Just one man ...

JEANNIE/FLORA.
YOU'RE THE ONLY ONE —

CLEO. ... at a time.

ALL.
— FOR ME.
YOU'RE THE ONLY ONE FOR ME!

(During the applause, Cleo cues the band and exits. The drummer plays a sharp machine gun riff.)

JEANNIE/FLORA. Uh-oh. *(Ben enters, dressed as a gangster, carrying a machine gun case. He saunters center and motions Jeannie and Flora over.)* Uh-oh. *(They edge nearer. Ben places the case in their hands and opens it.)* Uh-oh. *(Slowly, he takes out a smoking trumpet.)* Ohhhhhhhh! *(And we're into our second number — "CHICAGO STYLE.")*
HE GETS HIS SHIRTS STRAIGHT FROM PARIS,
CIGARETTES FROM THE NILE.
HE TALKS LIKE A HIGHBROW;

BEN.
BUT I PLAY CHICAGO STYLE.

JEANNIE/FLORA.

HE GETS HIS SHOES MADE IN LONDON
AND THEY'RE REAL CROCODILE;

BEN/JEANNIE/FLORA.

BUT I/HE PLAY/S TRUMPET CHICAGO STYLE!

JEANNIE/FLORA.

HE GETS HIS NECKTIES FROM NAPLES
AND HIS SOCKS FROM ARGYLL,
HE SPEAKS OXFORD ENGLISH;

BEN.

BUT I PLAY CHICAGO STYLE.

JEANNIE/FLORA.

HE WEARS A STICKPIN FROM RIO
YOU CAN SEE FOR A MILE;

BEN/JEANNIE/FLORA.

BUT I/HE PLAY/S TRUMPET CHICAGO STYLE.

JEANNIE/FLORA.

AND HE SOMETIMES PLAYS SWEET.

(Ben scats a riff.)

BUT SWEET OR HOT HE'S ALWAYS GOT
THAT REAL GUT BUCKET BEAT.
HE'S GOT A NEAT LATIN MUSTACHE

BEN.

AND THE GIRLS LOVE MY SMILE;

BEN/JEANNIE/FLORA.

BUT I/HE PLAY/S TRUMPET CHICAGO STYLE.

(The three do a hot Charleston — interrupted by the Waiter who dances on carrying a clarinet. The men circle each other, competing with fancy footwork. Jeannie and Flora join in. The Waiter gets a little carried away. Annoyed, Ben shoots him.)

BEN. Now, that's Chicago Style!

JEANNIE/FLORA.

AND HE SOMETIMES PLAYS SWEET.

(Ben scats a riff.)

BUT SWEET OR HOT HE'S ALWAYS GOT
THAT REAL GUT BUCKET BEAT.
HE LIKES NEW YORK FOR THE OP'RA.

BEN.

I GET TWO ON THE AISLE;

BEN/JEANNIE/FLORA.

BUT I/HE PLAY/S TRUMPET CHICAGO STYLE.
A TRUMPET MADE IN MUNICH PLAYED IN
CHICAGO STYLE!

(The performers bow and exit to a "CHICAGO STYLE" play-off. Ben spots Mame and motions the band to cut off.)

MAME. *(Laughing, to Reginald mid-conversation.)* ... Oh, Reggie, not really?

REGINALD. On my honor as a gentleman.

MAME. But what did you —

BEN. *(Interrupts.)* Do my glims glam onto a glob-a-honey? Mame, darlin'! I almost didn't recognize you. Where you been?

MAME. *(Shortly.)* Around. *(Back to Reginald.)* So, what did you do when they — *(Ben surreptitiously runs his finger lightly up her arm.)* Ben! *(Forced into this introduction.)* I'd like you to meet my fiancé, Sir Reginald —

BEN. *(Interrupts — to Reginald.)* Fian-saaay, didn't I used to see you here all the time, gettin' the lay of the land, so to speak? *(Before he can reply.)* Nice to meecha, Reggie. *(Ben comes back C. To audience.)* Folks, I am thrilled to announce that Mamie LaMarr — or Dora May to her friends — is back with us tonight. Mamie, of course, used to perform here — sometimes onstage — until she met Sir Reginald what's-his-name and gave up the business to give him the business. *(Big smile.)* Well, I am just heartsick. *(He cues the Band who play the intro to "AIN'T IT A SHAME ABOUT MAME.")*

BEN/(BAND).

BOYS, HAVE YOU HEARD THE NEWS?
(WHAT ABOUT? WHAT ABOUT?)
I JUST LOST MY GAL. AND BOY, WAS SHE A PAL.
(WHAT'S HER NAME? WHAT'S HER NAME?)
MAME IS HER NAME.

AIN'T IT A SHAME ABOUT MAME
(WHAT ABOUT HER?)
SHE HAS ONLY HERSELF TO BLAME.
(WHAT DID SHE DO?)
SHE CAN'T GO TO THE PICNICS AND HOOLIGAN'S GROVE.
(OHHHHHH?)
NO CORNED BEEF AND CABBAGE IS COOKED ON HER
        STOVE.
(NOOOOOO!)
SHE'LL MARRY SIR REGINALD WHAT'S-HIS-NAME?

(TOM, DICK, OR HARRY)

AIN'T IT A SHAME ABOUT MAME.

BEN. How 'bout helpin' me out up here, Mamie? For old time's sake?

MAME. No, thank you.

BAND. Aw, c'mon, Mame!

BEN. Now, honey, don't go gettin' shy on me. *(To audience.)* Mamie never used to be a shy one. I remember the night the Plumbers Local was here and —

MAME. — I'd love to join you. *(Mame joins him onstage. They immediately fall into one of their old dance patterns, a mixture of sashayin' and footwork.)*

MAME/(BEN).

THEY SAY, AIN'T IT A SHAME ABOUT MAME.
(YES, THEY DO!)
NOW SHE'S LOST ALL HER SPARK AND FLAME.
(SHE'S BURNIN' NOW!)
SHE HAS TO TALK FANCY AND EAT CAVIAR,
(LOVES HER CAVIAR!)
AND LOOK LIKE THOSE PICTURES IN HARPER'S BAZAAR.
(GRRRRRRRRRR!)
I'LL MARRY SIR REGINALD —
(WHAT'S HIS NAME?)

MAME/BEN.

AIN'T IT A SHAME ABOUT MAME.

BEN.

SHE HAS GOT TO BE SOCIAL.

MAME.

I HAVE TO GO TO THE NIGHT CLUBS.

BEN.

SHE HAS TO DANCE LIKE A CUBAN.

MAME.

BUT STILL ACT LIKE A LADY.

MAME/BEN.

OH, OH, OH, OH
YOU KNOW THIS DAME'S A LADY!

MAME.

I'LL MARRY SIR REGINALD —

BEN. What *is* his damn name?!

MAME. Ben!

BEN.

AIN'T IT A SHAME ABOUT —

MAME. *(To Ben.)*

I LOVES YA, HONEY
BUT'CHA GOT NO MONEY!

BEN.

SURE IS A SHAME ABOUT —

MAME.

NOW I GOT ME SOME CLASS

(Under her breath.)

SO GET OFFA MY ASS!

MAME/BEN.

AIN'T IT A SHAME ABOUT MAME!

(During the applause, Ben pulls Mame backstage.)

BEN. C'mon, Mame. Say hello to the gang.

MAME. *(Calls back to Reginald.)* You don't mind, do you, Reggie?

REGINALD. *(Standing.)* Well, I —

BEN. *(Calls off.)* Hey, Jeannie, table six needs a little company! *(Ben and Mame exit. From the other side we hear Jeannie's voice.)*

JEANNIE. *(Off.)* But Ben, I got a number to do. *(Jeannie emerges in her robe.)* Ben? *(She sighs, plasters a smile on her face and extends her hand as she turns to table six.)* Hello, I'm — *(Realizes it's Reginald.)* Oh! It's you!

REGINALD. Hello. *(He reaches to shake her hand, just as she withdraws it. Flustered, she extends it again — as he pulls back his. An awkward laugh. Embarrassed, they shake hands.)*

JEANNIE. ... I didn't see you before.

REGINALD. *(Smiles.)* You were busy.

JEANNIE. It's ... been awhile.

REGINALD. ... Yes, it has.

JEANNIE. So ... *(Fumbling for something to say, Jeannie sings "WHAT'S NEW.")*

WHAT'S NEW?
HOW IS THE WORLD TREATING YOU?
YOU HAVEN'T CHANGED A BIT;
HANDSOME AS EVER, I MUST ADMIT.

WHAT'S NEW?
HOW DID THAT ROMANCE COME THROUGH?
WE HAVEN'T MET SINCE THEN,
GEE! BUT IT'S NICE TO SEE YOU AGAIN.

WHAT'S NEW?
PROBABLY I'M BORING YOU,
BUT SEEING YOU IS GRAND,
AND YOU WERE SWEET TO OFFER YOUR HAND.

(Reginald looks over Jeannie's shoulder. Jeannie turns. Mame has entered from backstage and is watching them.)

... I UNDERSTAND.
ADIEU!

(The band picks up the melody as Jeannie backs away. Mame passes her. They briefly lock eyes. Mame indicates to Reginald she's ready to go. He follows her up the aisle — but can't bring himself to leave. Jeannie turns away, her back to the audience. The music builds, the lights change to a single spot. Jeannie drops her robe to reveal the backless dress underneath. She turns — a performer finishing her number.)

WHAT'S NEW?
PROBABLY I'M BORING YOU,
BUT SEEING YOU IS GRAND,
AND YOU WERE SWEET TO OFFER YOUR HAND ...

(She looks toward Reginald — a plea, a dare? — Mame puts her hand possessively on Reginald's arm. With a last look to Jeannie, he exits with Mame.)

I UNDERSTAND.
ADIEU!
PARDON MY ASKING WHAT'S NEW.
OF COURSE YOU COULDN'T KNOW,
I HAVEN'T CHANGED.

I STILL LOVE YOU SO!

(During the applause, Jeannie exits through the beaded curtains. Cleo appears from the other side. She sings "DOCTOR RHYTHM.")

CLEO.

WHO IS THE GREATEST BENEFACTOR OF MANKIND?
SOMEONE YOU'D NEVER REALIZE.
PERHAPS YOU'LL MEET HIM SOON.
SO KEEP HIS NAME IN MIND
BECAUSE HE DOESN'T ADVERTISE.

DOCTOR RHYTHM RUNS A CLINIC
WHERE ALL KINDS OF PEOPLE MEET,
WHERE A WEARY WORN OUT CYNIC
GETS BACK ON HIS FEET.

ARE YOU TROUBLED? DO YOU WONDER
WHY YOU'RE FILLED WITH DARK DESPAIR?
GO AND LOSE YOUR WORRIES UNDER
DOCTOR RHYTHM'S CARE.

AND IF IT'S A CASE
WHERE A HEARTACHE NEVER ENDS,
HE'LL FIX YOUR FACE
WITH A SMILE THAT MAKES NEW FRIENDS.

WHEN YOU THINK NO ONE CAN CURE YOU,
DOCTOR RHYTHM RATES A CHANCE,
WITH ONE TREATMENT HE'LL ASSURE YOU
LIFE IS JUST A DANCE!

(Ben dances on as "Doctor Rhythm." He seats the "ailing" Cleo in a chair and proceeds to "heal her." Tap break. Cleo slowly rises from the chair.)

WHEN YOU THINK NO ONE CAN CURE YOU,
DOCTOR RHYTHM RATES A CHANCE,
WITH ONE TREATMENT HE'LL ASSURE YOU
LIFE IS JUST A DANCE!

(As Ben taps around her.)

DOCTOR RHYTHM!
DOCTOR RHYTHM!
DOCTOR RHYTHM, HE'LL ASSURE YOU
LIFE IS JUST A DANCE!

(During the applause there is the sound of a siren.)

BEN. *(Running backstage.)* It's a raid!

CLEO. *(To the audience.)* Folks, folks! Don't panic! Stay calm! Everything's gonna be taken care of. *(Glaring at the "Senator.")* AIN'T THAT RIGHT, SENATOR!! *(Cleo hurries off as the Speakeasy recedes and we segue to ...)*

Scene 2

Time: 1929 — Late night.

Place: The Bowery — New York City.

A clap of thunder. It's cold and rainy. A Homeless Man, dressed in a threadbare jacket and scarf makes his way onto the stage. He warms his hands over a trashcan containing the smoldering remnants of a fire.

Another clap of thunder. The Man picks up a decrepit umbrella and opens it — nothing but spokes. He's about to toss it into the trashcan when something shiny falls from the umbrella to the ground. He bends down and picks up — a penny!

The Homeless Man smiles. He sings "PENNIES FROM HEAVEN."

HOMELESS MAN.

A LONG TIME AGO A MILLION YEARS B.C.
THE BEST THINGS IN LIFE WERE ABSOLUTELY FREE
BUT NO ONE APPRECIATED A SKY THAT WAS ALWAYS BLUE;
AND NO ONE CONGRATULATED A MOON THAT WAS ALWAYS NEW.
SO IT WAS PLANNED THAT THEY WOULD VANISH NOW AND THEN
AND YOU MUST PAY BEFORE YOU GET THEM BACK AGAIN;
THAT'S WHAT STORMS WERE MADE FOR,
AND YOU SHOULDN'T BE AFRAID FOR

EVERY TIME IT RAINS, IT RAINS,
PENNIES FROM HEAVEN.
DON'T YOU KNOW EACH CLOUD CONTAINS
PENNIES FROM HEAVEN?

YOU'LL FIND YOUR FORTUNE FALLING ALL OVER TOWN.
BE SURE THAT YOUR UMBRELLA IS UPSIDE DOWN.

TRADE THEM FOR A PACKAGE OF
SUNSHINE AND FLOWERS.

IF YOU WANT THE THINGS YOU LOVE,
YOU MUST HAVE SHOWERS.

SO WHEN YOU HEAR IT THUNDER DON'T RUN UNDER A TREE,
THERE'LL BE PENNIES FROM HEAVEN FOR YOU AND ME.

(Musical interlude. Four street people wearily drift on: The Junk Man with his peddler's cart. The Apple Seller with a cardboard tray that holds her unsold apples. The Homeless Woman with all her belongings tied in a bundle. The 2nd Homeless Woman carrying a torn shopping bag filled with rags. The Homeless Man watches as they settle in for the night.)

... YOU MUST HAVE SHOWERS.
SO WHEN YOU HEAR IT THUNDER DON'T RUN UNDER A TREE,
THERE'LL BE PENNIES FROM HEAVEN FOR YOU AND ME.

(After the applause the Polish Gentleman enters, slightly tipsy.)

POLISH GENTLEMAN. *(Singing.)*

ABOVE THE BROWNSTONES
THE MOON WAS BRIGHT,
AND ORCHARD AND DELANCEY
WERE ALL DRESSED UP —

STREET PEOPLE. Shhhh!/ Keep it down!/ It's late!/ We're trying to get some rest!

POLISH GENTLEMAN. *(Whispers the last lyric.)* — tonight. *(He approaches the Homeless Man.)* Congratulate me!

HOMELESS MAN. *(Politely.)* Congratulations.

POLISH GENTLEMAN. Thank you. You should see the bride. Beautiful!

HOMELESS MAN. The bride? Oh! *(Shakes his hand.)* Congratulations!

POLISH GENTLEMAN. Thank you.

HOMELESS MAN. *(Looks around.)* Where is she?

POLISH GENTLEMAN. Who?

HOMELESS MAN. The bride.

POLISH GENTLEMAN. Where should she be on her wedding night? With Stanislaus, of course!

HOMELESS MAN. *(Adrift.)* And Stanislaus is...?

POLISH GENTLEMAN. The groom, of course!

HOMELESS MAN. And I congratulated you because...?

POLISH GENTLEMAN. *(Happily.)* I'm not!

HOMELESS MAN. The groom.

POLISH GENTLEMAN. Of course! *(Confidentially.)* Beautiful, yes. But what a shrew! She's going to make his life a living hell!

HOMELESS MAN. Oh, well then … *(Shakes his hand again.)* Congratulations!

POLISH GENTLEMAN. Thank you. *(Rhapsodizing.)* Ah, what a wedding! *(He breaks into song.)*

WE DRANK ALL THE WINE
WHEN STANISLAUS GOT MARRIED,
I HAD EIGHT OR NINE
AND COULDN'T SEE THE DOOR.

OGLESKI DID THE POLKA WITH EMILY HOMOLKA,
ZULTOWSKI TRIED TO FOLLOW THEM
BUT COULDN'T FIND THE FLOOR.

WE DRANK ALL THE WINE
WHEN STANISLAUS GOT MARRIED,
I HAD EIGHT OR NINE
AND STOOD IN LINE FOR MORE.

(The Homeless Man pats him on the shoulder and begins to walk away. Grabs his arm.)

KUBACHYK SANG MAZURKAS
WITH KACHMAREK AND FRANKOWSKI.
MULAVA WAS CRYING AND
KOVALSKI FELT A GLOW,

BUT NOVACK JOINED THE ARGUMENT
WITH KUDLICK AND DOMBROWSKI,
THAT STARTED WHEN POLESIE
STEPPED ON LUBOMICSKI'S TOE.

SO, DUDEK PICKED A TABLE UP
AND THREW IT AT OVOCKI.
KOKOVICH TOLD VATZEK
THAT HIS HEAD WAS MADE OF WOOD.

ZWOLINSKI TACKLED YANEK
AND THE HOUSE WAS GETTING ROCKY.
THE BRIDE AND GROOM WERE HAPPY
'CAUSE THE WEDDING WENT SO GOOD!

(The band continues vamping.)

STREET PEOPLE. Quiet!/ It's late!/ Go home!

HOMELESS WOMAN. Aaah, he's drunk!

POLISH GENTLEMAN. *(Indignant.)* Drunk! My good woman, could a drunk man do this? *(He does an intricate tap break.)*

HOMELESS WOMAN. *(Impressed.)* That was good.

POLISH GENTLEMAN. *(Already forgot.)* What was?

HOMELESS WOMAN. *(To others.)* Drunk.

POLISH GENTLEMAN. *(Indignant.)* Drunk! I'll show you drunk! *(Calling off.)* Leopold, faster!

HOMELESS MAN. Leopold?

POLISH GENTLEMAN. My conductor.

HOMELESS MAN. What's a band doing on the streets of the Bowery?

POLISH GENTLEMAN. *(Aside.)* You think that's strange, look at the guy in the third row. *(Calling.)* Leopold, faster! *(The band vamps faster. A big breath.)*

KUBACHYK SANG MAZURKAS
WITH KACHMAREK AND FRANKOWSKI.
MULAVA WAS CRYING AND
KOVALSKI FELT A GLOW,

BUT NOVACK JOINED THE ARGUMENT
WITH KUDLICK AND DOMBROWSKI,
THAT STARTED WHEN POLESIE
STEPPED ON LUBOMICSKI'S TOE.

SO, DUDEK PICKED A TABLE ...

(The band vamps as he looks out into the house.) You think this is easy? You, the strange one in the third row. *(Calling.)* House lights!

HOMELESS MAN. *(As the house lights come up.)* House lights?

POLISH GENTLEMAN. *(Shrugs.)* Hey, if I can have a conductor I can have house lights. *(Yells offstage.)* Leopold! Stop-o-vich! *(The band cuts off. He steps down into the house. To a man in the third row.)* And how are you, sir? *(The man will probably say "fine ...")*

Yeah? Not for long. Trust me, this won't be painless. Now, repeat. *(He leads the man through the lyrics.)*

KUBACHYK SANG MAZURKAS
WITH KACHMAREK AND FRANKOWSKI.

(The man repeats. The Polish Gentleman continues.)

MULAVA WAS CRYING AND
KOVALSKI FELT A GLOW,

(The man starts to repeat.) No, no no. *(Holding the man's jaw — helping him shape the word.)* Mulava. Moooo. Mooooo. Moooolava. *(The man tries.)* I think he needs help. *(To audience member next to the man.)* You busy? *(He leads them* both *in the lyric. Holding both their jaws — helping them shape the word.)* Mulava. Moooo. Mooooo. Moooolava. *(To audience.)* We need more help. We need to see the words. *(Calls up.)* Give me a sign! *(We hear a clap of thunder.)* Not a sign! A sign!! *(The Street People run to the junk cart and pull out a bunch of signs, each with a different line from the song. They line up at the foot of the stage.)* Now ... *(He leads the audience as they recite.)*

ALL/AUDIENCE.

KUBACHYK SANG MAZURKAS
WITH KACHMAREK AND FRANKOWSKI.
MULAVA WAS CRYING AND
KOVALSKI FELT A GLOW,
BUT NOVACK JOINED THE ARGUMENT
WITH KUDLICK AND DOMBROWSKI,
THAT STARTED WHEN POLESIE
STEPPED ON LUBOMICSKI'S TOE.

POLISH GENTLEMAN. Not bad.... Not good, but not bad. Let's try it with music. *(Calls off.)* Leopold, resume-a-vich! *(He waits. No music.)* Leopold, you son-a-vich! Resume-a-vich! *(The band plays an introductory chord. The Polish Gentleman leads the audience in a sing-a-long.)*

ALL/AUDIENCE.

KUBACHYK SANG MAZURKAS
WITH KACHMAREK AND FRANKOWSKI.
MULAVA WAS CRYING AND
KOVALSKI FELT A GLOW,

BUT NOVACK JOINED THE ARGUMENT
WITH KUDLICK AND DOMBROWSKI,
THAT STARTED WHEN POLESIE
STEPPED ON LUBOMICSKI'S TOE.

(The Polish Gentleman joins the others on stage as the band modulates and everyone repeats.)

ALL.

KUBACHYK SANG MAZURKAS
WITH KACHMAREK AND FRANKOWSKI.
MULAVA WAS CRYING AND
KOVALSKI FELT A GLOW,

BUT NOVACK JOINED THE ARGUMENT
WITH KUDLICK AND DOMBROWSKI,
THAT STARTED WHEN POLESIE
STEPPED ON LUBOMICSKI'S TOE.

(They all dance off — and dance right back on, now wearing large Russian hats!)

SO DUDEK PICKED A TABLE UP
AND THREW IT AT OVOCKI,
KOKOVICH TOLD VATZEK
THAT HIS HEAD WAS MADE OF WOOD.

ZWOLINSKI TACKLED YANEK
AND THE HOUSE WAS GETTING ROCKY,
THE BRIDE AND GROOM WERE HAPPY
'CAUSE THE WEDDING WENT SO GOOD!

THE BRIDE AND GROOM WERE HAPPY
'CAUSE THE WEDDING WENT SO GOOD!

(After the applause, a Housewife opens the door of one of the decaying brownstones.)

HOUSEWIFE. *(To the others.)* Excuse me. Could you keep it down? My baby's sleeping.

STREET PEOPLE. *(Whispering.)* Sorry. *(They exit. The Housewife picks up a child's rocking horse. Wearily, she sinks down onto the stoop and sings "HIS ROCKING HORSE RAN AWAY.")*

HOUSEWIFE.

I MUST SIT DOWN FOR A MINUTE,
I'M READY TO FALL IN A HEAP.
WILLIE'S BEEN FED. AND I'VE TUCKED HIM IN BED;
THANK GOODNESS THE DARLING'S ASLEEP.
HE'S A WONDERFUL BOY AND A JOY AND A BOON,
BUT OH, YOU SHOULD HAVE SEEN HIM THIS AFTERNOON.

BANG! WENT THE BRIDGE LAMP,
DOWN WENT THE TABLE,
CRASH! WENT THE CHINA TRAY,
BUT HE REALLY COULDN'T HELP IT,
HIS ROCKING HORSE RAN AWAY.

RIP! RIP! WENT THE CURTAIN
WHAM! WENT THE WINDOW,

CRUNCH! WENT THE NEW BUFFET
AND I HEARD HIM TELL HIS DADDY
"MY ROCKING HORSE RAN AWAY."

SOMEHOW INDIANS GOT INTO OUR FRONT ROOM.
OUR COWBOY GRABBED FOR HIS GUN AND WENT
BOOM! BOOM! BOOM! BOOM! BOOM!

SLAM! WENT THE SCREEN DOOR,
SMASH! WENT THE MIRROR,
LOOKS LIKE I'LL SOON BE GRAY,
BUT HE SMILES AND WHAT'S THE DIFFERENCE;
AND MAYBE SOME MOTHER'S DAY
I'LL REMEMBER WHEN HIS ROCKING HORSE RAN AWAY.

CAME HOME LATE FROM A PICTURE.
I WAS TIRED. MY SHOES WERE TIGHT.
TOOK OFF MY STOCKINGS. DROPPED MY GIRDLE.
GOT UNDRESSED AND PULLED THE LIGHT, BOY!

SLIPPED INTO MY NIGHTGOWN
THEN TIP-TOED ACROSS THE FLOOR.
BETTER HAVE A LOOK AT JUNIOR.
SO I PEEKED INTO HIS DOOR.

CLANG! WENT A COWBELL!
WHEEE! WENT A WHISTLE!
I NEARLY HAD A STROKE!
IT WAS MOTHER'S PRECIOUS BABY
JUST HAVIN' HIS LITTLE JOKE.

ALWAYS JUST WHEN I'M BREATHIN' A BIG FULL SIGH
THERE'S G-MEN, COPPERS AND ROBBERS
AND HIGH HO SILVER!

BAM! WENT THE BOOKCASE!
FOOMP! WENT THE FRUIT BOWL
GLUMP! WENT THE GLASS BOUQUET.

BUT HE SMILES AND WHAT'S THE DIFFERENCE
AND MAYBE SOME MOTHER'S DAY
I'LL REMEMBER WHEN —

BANG! WENT THE LAMP!
DOWN! WENT THE TABLE!
CRASH! WENT THE TRAY!
RIP! RIP! WENT THE CURTAIN!
WHAM! WENT A WINDOW!
CLANG! WENT A BELL!
WHEEE! WENT A WHISTLE
BAM! WENT A PAN!
SLAM! WENT A DOOR!
ON THAT EVENTFUL DAY!
WHEN HIS ROCKING HORSE RAN AWAY!

(The Houswife goes back inside. Man 1 enters in a green checkered suit, carrying a bouquet of flowers. He approaches the brownstone door and rings the bell. No answer. He starts to leave when he sees — Man 2 enter, in a yellow checkered suit, carrying a box of candy. He approaches the door and knocks. No answer. He, too, starts to leave when he sees — Man 3 enter, in a red checkered suit, carrying candy and *flowers. He approaches the door and simultaneously knocks and rings the bell. No answer. He starts to leave when he sees the other two. The Men circle each other suspiciously. They inch closer. A fight seems imminent. Abruptly, they turn to the audience and sing "ANNIE DOESN'T LIVE HERE ANYMORE.")*

MAN 3.

HERE'S A TRAGEDY THAT HAPPENED ON A SIDE STREET,

MAN 1.

WHEN A FELLOW WENT TO RING HIS SWEETHEART'S BELL.

MAN 2.

HE SAW THE SHADES WERE DRAWN,
AND HE KNEW HIS GAL WAS GONE,

MEN.

WHEN HE LISTENED TO THE STORY,
THAT A NEIGHBOR HAD TO TELL.

(The Housewife sticks her head out her window.)

HOUSEWIFE. *(Yelling.)* Annie doesn't live here anymore!! *(She slams down the window. The Men turn to the audience.)*

MEN.

OH, ANNIE DOESN'T LIVE HERE ANYMORE,
YOU MUST BE THE ONE SHE WAITED FOR.
SHE SAID I WOULD KNOW YOU BY THE BLUE IN YOUR EYE,
CHECKERED SUIT, A FANCY VEST, AND POLKA-DOT TIE.
YOU ANSWER TO THAT DESCRIPTION,
SO I GUESS THAT YOU'RE THE GUY,
WELL, ANNIE DOESN'T LIVE HERE ANYMORE.

ANNIE DOESN'T LIVE HERE ANYMORE,
IT'S TOO BAD YOU DIDN'T CALL BEFORE.
SHE JUST BOUGHT A GOWN THAT TIES WITH RIBBONS ABOVE,
BRAND NEW SHOES, A PRETTY HAT AND LATEST STYLE GLOVE.
SHE REALLY LOOKED SO ALLURING,
AND JUST WAITING FOR YOUR LOVE,
BUT ANNIE DOESN'T LIVE HERE ANYMORE.

IT WAS SPRING,
THERE WAS ROMANCE IN THE AIR,
AND EV'RYTHING
SEEMED FOR LOVING HEARTS TO SHARE,
AND THERE WAS SHE,
JUST AS LONELY AND AS BLUE
AS SHE COULD BE;
THAT'S THE REASON

ANNIE DOESN'T LIVE HERE ANYMORE.
MIGHT HAVE BEEN YOUR PICTURE THAT SHE TORE,
SHE WAS OH SO FAITHFUL, WHAT A PITIFUL SIGHT,
WAITED FOR THE LETTER THAT YOU PROMISED TO WRITE.
A GENTLEMAN WITH A TOP HAT
CALLED AROUND THE OTHER NIGHT,
AND ANNIE DOESN'T LIVE HERE ANYMORE.

(Woman 2 and 3 enter upstage. During the following, the Men help Man 3 reverse his jacket and rip off the break-away checkered pants to reveal his other suit.)

ALL.

OH, ANNIE DOESN'T LIVE HERE ANYMORE,
YOU MUST BE THE ONE SHE WAITED FOR.

SHE SAID I WOULD KNOW YOU BY THE BLUE IN YOUR EYE,
CHECKERED SUIT, A FANCY VEST, AND POLKA-DOT TIE.

(Man 1 and 2 exit as the Women join Man 3 to become "The Harmonics.")

THE HARMONICS.

YOU ANSWER TO THAT DESCRIPTION,
SO I GUESS THAT YOU'RE THE GUY,
WELL, ANNIE DOESN'T LIVE HERE ANYMORE.

(The Harmonics continue singing, spotlighted around a center microphone as the bandstand rolls on and the set begins to change.)

ANNIE WAS FAITHFUL.
ANNIE WAS TRUE.
ANNIE WAS LOYAL
BUT WHAT COULD SHE DO?

YOU NEVER CAME BY.
YOU NEVER SAID WHY.
YOU LEFT HER ALONE
AND YOU MADE ANNIE CRY.

NOW YOU'RE CRYING TOO.
BOO-HOO!

(During the following, Man 1 & 2 re-enter with Woman 1 — dressed for their roles in the radio show. The Harmonics continue singing while the others set up their microphones.)

IT WAS SPRING,
THERE WAS ROMANCE IN THE AIR,
AND EV'RYTHING
SEEMED FOR LOVING HEARTS TO SHARE,

AND THERE WAS SHE,
JUST AS LONELY AND AS BLUE
AS SHE COULD BE;
THAT'S THE REASON

(The tempo doubles as the lights change and we segue to ...)

Scene 3

Time: 1935 — Afternoon

Place: Radio Show — New York City

A radio broadcast.

Overhead is a large clock surrounded by the logo, "YOUR HIT PARADE." On separate sides hang the "On the Air" and "Applause" signs.

The Harmonics are now joined vocally by the Announcer (Man 1) and Buddy and Betty — America's Sweethearts, (Man 2/Woman 1).

ALL.

ANNIE DOESN'T LIVE HERE ANYMORE.

HARMONICS.

OH, NO, SHE DOESN'T LIVE HERE.

ALL.

MIGHT HAVE BEEN YOUR PICTURE THAT SHE TORE,

HARMONICS.

INTO A MILLION PIECES.

ALL.

SHE WAS OH SO FAITHFUL,

HARMONICS.

WHAT A PITIFUL SIGHT,

ALL.

WAITED FOR THE LETTER

HARMONICS.

THAT YOU PROMISED TO WRITE.

ALL.

A GENTLEMAN WITH A TOP HAT
CALLED AROUND THE OTHER NIGHT,
AND ANNIE DOESN'T LIVE HERE ANYMORE.

ANNOUNCER. *("Yeth sir!")* She packed her suitcase!

ALL.

ANNIE DOESN'T LIVE HERE ANYMORE.

BUDDY. And moved to Jersey!

ALL.

ANNIE DOESN'T LIVE HERE ANYMORE!

(The Announcer motions the audience to clap as the "Applause" sign flashes. NOTE: the actors read all their dialogue from radio scripts.)

ANNOUNCER. Yes, that was "Annie Doesn't Live Here Anymore," number five on this week's Hit Parade. And a very special Hit Parade it is as we celebrate —

HARMONICS. *(Singing his name.)*

"JOHNNY BURKE."

ANNOUNCER. — the only man to have five songs in the Hit Parade at the same time. As always, today's countdown will be performed by our regulars, The Harmonics —

HARMONICS. *(Singing.)*

"HI, BOB!"

ANNOUNCER. And, of course, America's Sweethearts — Buddy and Betty!

BUDDY. Hi, Bob!

ANNOUNCER. Hi, Buddy!

BETTY. Hi, Bob!

ANNOUNCER. Hi, Betty! *(Big build up.)* And, also, our very special guest, Hollywood's favorite female — Vicky Voyay! *(Big fanfare. They all face upstage. Nothing. Covering.)* Who's flying in even as we speak. *(Skipping in the script — the others try to catch up.)* Say, Buddy and Betty, we've been getting mountains of mail from our listeners wondering —

1ST HARMONIC. "When did you two meet?"

2ND HARMONIC. "Where did you two meet?"

3RD HARMONIC. "How did you two meet?"

BUDDY. Well, why don't we skip the meat and get right to the potatoes?

HARMONICS. *(From script.)* Ha ha ha.

ANNOUNCER. Buddy, you're a caution! Seriously, how *did* you two meet?

BETTY. Well, Bob, actually it was a year ago today, right here at the theatre. We were both waiting to audition for the show and I was very nervous and Buddy said —

BUDDY. "You seem very nervous."

BETTY. Right away I was struck by his sensitivity. And I said, "I am very nervous." And he said —

BUDDY. "Don't be." *(A beat. The others wait for Buddy to continue. Nothing. Everyone hurriedly checks their scripts to see if it's their line.)*

ANNOUNCER. *(Jumping in with his cue.)* Well, that must have put you at ease.

BETTY. It certainly did! I don't think I've ever sung as well as I sang that day.

BUDDY. I'll say! *(Betty shoots him a look, not certain how to take that.)*

BETTY. And that's how I got the job.

BUDDY. And I got Betty!

HARMONICS. *(Scripted.)* Awwwwwww.

BETTY. *(Coyly.)* Well, not right away. I did play hard-to-get.

BUDDY. That's right. She didn't say "yes" 'til I got through asking.

HARMONICS. *(From script.)* Ha ha ha.

ANNOUNCER. Buddy, you're a stitch! Now how 'bout singin' the next song?

BUDDY. Love to, Bob!

ANNOUNCER. Okay, folks, off we go with Buddy and his — "Scatterbrain!"

(The Announcer goes off to find Vicky as the Harmonics sing —)

HARMONICS. *(Singing.)*

"NUMBER FOUR."

(Buddy sings "SCATTER-BRAIN.")

BUDDY.

EV'RYONE WHO SEES YOU SAYS "FASCINATING FACE,"
"HEAVENS WHAT A FIGURE," AND "GOODNESS ME WHAT GRACE."
EV'RYONE WHO MEETS YOU MUST LOSE HIS HEART I FIND,
THEN HE'S SURE TO LOSE HIS MIND.

BETTY. Oh, Buddy.

BUDDY.

YOU'RE AS PLEASANT AS THE MORNING
AND REFRESHING AS THE RAIN,
ISN'T IT A PITY THAT YOU'RE SUCH A SCATTER-BRAIN?

WHEN YOU SMILE IT'S SO DELIGHTFUL,
WHEN YOU TALK IT'S SO INSANE,
STILL IT'S CHARMING CHATTER, SCATTER-BRAIN.

BETTY. *(Same.)* Oh, Buddy.

BUDDY.

I KNOW I'LL END UP APOPLECTIC
BUT THERE'S NOTHING I CAN DO.
IT'S JUST THE SAME AS BEING
IN A HURRICANE.
AND THOUGH MY LIFE WILL BE
TOO HECTIC, I'M SO MUCH IN
LOVE WITH YOU.

BETTY

I don't think it's very nice to call someone a scatterbrain. I may be a little forgetful but who isn't. I mean everyone has their faults and I don't go around pointing out your imperfections although I certainly could if I chose to but I don't so I won't.

NOTHING ELSE CAN MATTER Buddy —
NOTHING ELSE CAN MATTER Buddy —
NOTHING ELSE CAN MATTER
YOU'RE MY DARLING SCATTER-BRAIN!

HARMONICS. *(Singing.)*

"NUMBER THREE. NUMBER THREE ..."

BETTY. Oh, Buddy, you make me so mad. I just have to count to ten. *(In tempo.)* One, two, three, four, five, six, seven, eight, nine, ten. Awwww — *(Betty sings "ONE, TWO, BUTTON YOUR SHOE.")*

ONE, TWO, BUTTON YOUR SHOE,
PUT ON YOUR COAT AND HAT;
I PLAY A GAME LIKE THAT
WHILE I'M WAITING FOR YOU.

THREE, FOUR, OPEN THE DOOR,
HURRY FOR HEAVEN'S SAKE;
I COUNT EACH STEP YOU TAKE
WHILE I'M WAITING FOR YOU.

FIVE, SIX, MY HEART DOES TRICKS
AS I PICTURE ALL YOUR CHARMS.
SEVEN, EIGHT, YOU'RE AT THE GATE
AND YOU WALK INTO MY ARMS.

NINE, TEN, KISS ME AGAIN,
TELL ME YOU GET A THRILL;
JUST AS I HOPE YOU WILL
WHILE I'M WAITING FOR YOU.

(Dance break finish. The Announcer runs on. He motions to the others that Vicky has arrived. They hurry to their mikes.)

ANNOUNCER. And now, ladies and gentlemen, as we promised you, all the way from Hollywood, our very special guest — Vicky Voyay! *(Big fanfare! All turn upstage. Nothing. Covering.)* — will be here shortly! I understand her plane has just landed and — *(Vicky Voyay enters — gorgeous, sexy, dumb.)*

VICKY. *(Blithely.)* Hi, Bob!

ANNOUNCER. *(Not missing a beat.)* — luckily the airport is right next door. *(Turning to her.)* Why if it isn't Vicky Voyay!

VICKY. *(Confused.)* No, Bob, it is. It is Vicky Voyay.

ANNOUNCER. Uh, right. So, Vicky, I understand you have a new movie coming out.

VICKY. *(This girl plays the house.)* That's right, Bob. And I want to thank all my fans for making it such a big hit.

ANNOUNCER. Oh, it opened already.

VICKY. *(Pleased.)* Did it?

ANNOUNCER. *(A beat — moving on.)* Well, Vicky, as you know, we're honoring a very special songwriter, today. Johnny Burke.

VICKY. *(Enthusiastically.)* I know! *(Looks out at the audience and throws her arms open wide.)* Johnny, come on up!

ANNOUNCER. Uh, no, Vicky, Johnny's not here, today.

VICKY. *(Disappointed.)* Ohhhhhhhh, dear, dear, dear.

ANNOUNCER. But he's got the Top Five songs in our Hit Parade this week and we're thrilled that you came all this way to sing one of them.

VICKY. *(Concerned.)* No, no, no. I'm singing "What Does It Take To Make You Take To Me."

ANNOUNCER. Yes, he wrote that.

VICKY. *(Amazing coincidence.)* Did he?!

ANNOUNCER. *(An introduction.)* Ladies and Gentlemen, here's Vicky Voyay to answer the musical question, "What Does it Take."

VICKY. *(Answering.)* Lots of voice lessons and use your diagram. *(The Announcer gives up. He cues the Harmonics.)*

HARMONICS. *(Singing.)*

"NUMBER TWO."

(Vicky sings "WHAT DOES IT TAKE TO MAKE YOU TAKE TO ME.")

VICKY. *(Extremely sexy.)*

IT TAKES AN EARTHQUAKE TO MOVE A MOUNTAIN,
IT TAKES A TYPHOON TO CHURN UP THE SEA.
BUT WHAT DOES IT TAKE
TO MAKE YOU TAKE TO ME?

(Vicky moves around the mike to say hello to her fans. She turns back to the mike to sing, only now she's facing upstage.)

IT TAKES A HEAT WAVE TO MELT AN ICEBERG,
IT TAKES A BLOSSOM TO BOTHER A BEE.

(The others motion her to move around the mike and face the audience.)

BUT WHAT DOES IT TAKE
TO MAKE YOU TAKE TO ME?

(Mouthing her "choreography," she steps back and front.) And back and front. *(During the following, one of Vicky's false eyelashes begins to bother her.)*

YOU COULD HAVE YOUR WAY,
YOU COULD HAVE THE MOON,
ANYTHING YOU SAY,
ONLY SAY IT SOON.

(The eyelash becomes so irritating she takes it off. Now the gluey lash is stuck to her glove. She tries to shake it loose.)

WHEN YOU'RE AROUND
IT TAKES A FEATHER TO KNOCK ME OVER,
IT TAKES A NITWIT TO TELL YOU I'M FREE.

(She ineptly applies it back to her own eyelash where it dangles limply.)

'CAUSE BABY I'M JUST YOUR HUMBLE SERVANT,
MAKING THIS FERVENT PLEA:
BUT WHAT DOES IT TAKE
TO MAKE YOU TAKE TO ME?

(Vicky throws off her wrap. The Men rush forward vying to put it back on her. This turns into a tug-of-war with Vicky in the middle. The wraps ends up around her head. She manages to extricate herself in time to sing.)

WHEN YOU'RE AROUND
IT TAKES A FEATHER —

(The men now realize they're just standing there and become an ad-hoc back-up group.)

MEN.

OOO — OOO.

VICKY.

TO KNOCK ME OVER,

MEN.

AHH — AHH.

VICKY.

IT TAKES A —

MEN.

NITWIT —

VICKY.

TO TELL YOU I'M FREE,

MEN.

SO FREE!

VICKY.

— 'CAUSE BABY I'M JUST YOUR HUMBLE SERVANT,
MAKING THIS FERVENT PLEA:

MEN. Please!

VICKY.

BUT WHAT DOES IT TAKE
TO MAKE YOU TAKE TO ME?

MEN.

TO HER.

VICKY.

TO ME.

MEN.

TO HER.

VICKY. *(Getting mixed up.)*

TO HER.

MEN. *(Correcting her.)*

TO YOU.

VICKY.

TO YOU?

MEN.

"TO ME."

VICKY.

TO ME?

MEN.

YES!!

VICKY.

YES!!

(During the applause, as Vicky drifts upstage, her wrap gets caught on the microphone stand. The stand almost crashes to the floor but the Announcer catches it. He hands Vicky a script while the Harmonics sing "IRRESISTIBLE.")

HARMONICS.

IRRESISTIBLE.
YOU WERE FURTHEST FROM MY MIND
AND THEN WE MET;
AND NOW MY PLANS ARE ALL UPSET.
CAN I FEEL SECURE
KNOWING WELL THAT YOU'RE
IRRESISTIBLE?

VICKY. *(To Harmonics.)* Thank you.

ANNOUNCER. *(Reading from script.)* Say, Vicky, can I ask you something?

VICKY. *(Flat reading — as if it's a stage direction.)* Shoot Bob. *(The Announcer whispers in her ear.)* Oh! *(As in "go ahead.")* Shoot, Bob!

ANNOUNCER. Well, Vicky. How is it you always smell so gosh darn good?

VICKY. *(Reading.)* Oh, Bob, I can't give away my secrets. Especially when we're in the air.

ANNOUNCER. *(Keep that smile.)* We're *on* the air.

VICKY. *(And so pleased.)* I know! *(Taps microphone — to the listeners at home.)* Hellloooooo.

ANNOUNCER. *(Quickly back to script.)* Oh, c'mon Vicky. Just a hint. I'm sure our female listeners are dying to know.

VICKY. Well, alright. My secret is Irritable Perfume. *(Announcer whispers in her ear. Correcting herself.)* Irre*sis*tible Perfume. *(To Harmonics.)* I *thought* that sounded strange. Who would buy irritable perfume?

ANNOUNCER. *(Trying — though the ship is sinking.)* So, your secret is *Irresistible* Perfume, is it? I should have guessed. I hear all the really big movie stars are wearing it.

VICKY. Well, only the women. *(Beat — confidentially.)* Although I did hear that John Barrymore —

ANNOUNCER. *(Quickly.)* Vicky! Vicky! Vicky! In conclusion, is there anything more you'd like to tell us about Irresistible Perfume?

VICKY. *(Reading.)* Pick up a bottle of Irre*sis*tible Perfume — *(Visibly pleased she got it right.)* — for those nights when you're feeling a morous. *(To Announcer.)* Who's Morris?

ANNOUNCER. *(Is there a God?)* Well, Vicky, on behalf of our studio audience and all the people at home, we want to thank you so much for stopping by.

VICKY. *(Ever gracious.)* Thank you.

ANNOUNCER. But we know you *have* to go.

VICKY. I do?

ANNOUNCER. *(Firmly.)* You do. *(The Announcer cues the Harmonics.)*

HARMONICS

"NUMBER ONE.
NUMBER ONE."

(They repeat.)

VICKY. *(Into microphone.)* Bye-bye.

ANNOUNCER. *(Gently sidles Vicky away from the mike.)* And now, folks, we're going to wrap up this week's countdown.

HARMONICS.

THIS SONG IS NUMBER ONE!

(As the others get in place for the number, Vicky bids good-bye to the audience and exits.)

ANNOUNCER. Yes, it's the number one song in the country as Johnny Burke takes us back to school with, "AN APPLE FOR THE TEACHER."

(All sing "AN APPLE FOR THE TEACHER.")

WOMEN.

ONCE UPON A TIME
THERE WAS A BOY WHO WENT TO SCHOOL.
HE NEVER KNEW HIS LESSONS
AND HE SEEMED AN AWFUL FOOL,

HE NEVER LEARNED ADDITION
OR THE WAY TO MULTIPLY.
BUT BY PECULIAR METHODS
HE WOULD MANAGE TO GET BY.

HOW WE'LL NEVER KNOW!

(Vicky re-enters upstage, having gone off the wrong way. She tip-toes across stage, indicating to the audience, "I'm not here.")

MEN.

I GOT AN APPLE FOR THE TEACHER.
THAT SEEMS THE THING TO DO
BECAUSE I WANT TO LEARN ABOUT
ROMANCE FROM YOU.

A LITTLE APPLE FOR THE TEACHER
TO SHOW I'M MEEK AND MILD,
IF YOU INSIST ON SAYING THAT I'M
JUST A PROBLEM CHILD.

(Liking the number, Vicky decides to join the others — and proceeds to get in everyone's way.)

WOMEN.

YOU'LL GET ALL MY ATTENTION.

MEN.

YOUR WISH WILL BE MY RULE.

WOMEN.

AND MAYBE I'LL BE GOOD TO YOU

MEN.

AND KEEP ME, AFTER SCHOOL.
AN APPLE FOR THE TEACHER
THAT'S HOW I'D LIKE TO START,

THEN AFTER A WHILE YOU MAY GIVE IN
AND LET ME BRING MY HEART.

WOMEN.

OH, YOU THINK YOU'RE SMART
AND YOU KNOW ALL THE ANSWERS.
WELL, YOU CAN'T FOOL US
WE KNOW YOU'RE NOT A SAINT.

BUT YOU ALWAYS HAVE YOUR WAY.
SO, THERE'S NOTHING WE CAN SAY
BUT WHAT THE HECK
DO YOU GOT THAT WE AIN'T?!

MEN. Well —

I GOT AN APPLE FOR THE TEACHER.

WOMEN

IT'LL ALWAYS DO THE TRICK,

ALL.

WHEN YOU DON'T KNOW YOUR LESSON IN ARITHMETIC.
AN APPLE FOR THE TEACHER
WILL MEET WITH GREAT SUCCESS,
IF YOU FORGET TO MEMORIZE
THE GETTYSBURG ADDRESS.

VICKY. *(Prompted by the Announcer.)*

A LITTLE BIT OF GLAMOUR,

BETTY/BUDDY.

A CHARM THAT'S CUTE AND QUAINT;

ANNOUNCER.

AND SHE'LL EXCUSE YOUR GRAMMAR

HARMONICS.

AND BELIEVE YOU'RE WHAT YOU AIN'T.

ALL.

YOU MAY BE JUST A LEMON,
BUT SHE'LL THINK YOU'RE A PEACH,
JUST BRING AN APPLE FOR THE TEACHER
WHEN SHE STARTS TO TEACH.

HARMONICS. *(Singing.)*

BY-BYE!
BY-BYE!

ANNOUNCER. We'll be here next week, folks. Same time, same station on your dial. Until then —

HARMONICS. Think of us —

BUDDY/BETTY. 'Cause we'll be —

ANNOUNCER. Thinking of — *(They look expectantly to Vicky to finish with "You.")*

VICKY. *(Stumped.)* — Sounds like...?

ALL. *(Giving up — this one is a lemon.)*

YOU MAY BE JUST A LEMON,

(Back to audience.)

BUT SHE'LL THINK YOU'RE A PEACH,
JUST BRING AN APPLE FOR THE TEACHER
WHEN SHE STARTS TO TEACH.

VICKY. *(Finally getting it.)* Ohhhh, "Thinking of *you!*" *(And on that small step for mankind we — Blackout.)*

Transition to Scene 4

*We see a projection of a radio tower sending out pulsing sound waves as we hear the constant beep of a teletype. NOTE: The following voices can be pre-recorded by Man 1, 2 and 3.**

WALTER WINCHELL. *(V.O.)* Good evening Mr. and Mrs. North and South America and all the ships and clippers at sea. Let's go to press. Flash ... *(Radio static.)*

ANNOUNCER. *(V.O.)* ... from the British capital by Edward R. Murrow. Go ahead London.

EDWARD R. MURROW. *(V.O.)* This is London. The raids last night ... *(Radio static.)*

ANNOUNCER. *(V.O. Musical fanfare.)* Stage Door Canteen! Curtain up for Victory! *(The musical fanfare is interrupted by:)*

NEWS ANNOUNCER. *(V.O.)* — We interrupt this program to bring you a special news bulletin ... *(Radio static.)*

ANNOUNCER. *(V.O.)* ... General Dwight D. Eisenhour.

DWIGHT D. EISENHOWER. *(V.O.)* A landing was made this morning on the coast of France ... *(Radio static.)*

* See Author's Note in back of book.

WALTER WINCHELL. *(V.O.)* Attention, chorus girls. The USO camp shows want two hundred chorus girls ... *(Radio static. We hear the tinny strains of a swing band and the USO MC singing "THANK YOUR LUCKY STARS AND STRIPES.")*

MC. *(V.O.)*

IF YOU LIVE RIGHT,
IF YOU GET TO SLEEP AT NIGHT,
YOU CAN THANK YOUR LUCKY STARS AND STRIPES.

IF YOU FEEL FREE,
IF THERE'S SUGAR IN YOUR TEA,
YOU CAN THANK YOUR LUCKY STARS AND STRIPES ...

ANNOUNCER. *(V.O. over MC's singing.)* And now, ladies and gentlemen, coming to you live from our Allied Headquarters in the Pacific Islands — it's a USO All Star Special! *(And the lights come up to reveal ...)*

Scene 4

Time: 1944 — Day.

Place: Uso Show — Pacific Islands.

A USO show being performed live on an airbase in the Pacific. The show's MC sings into a microphone.

MC.

STEAM HEAT AND HAM AND EGGS,
AND HAY RIDES AND CIDER KEGS;
IF YOU LIKE THE GOOD OLD YANKEE WAY SO,
SAY SO.

(Yells out front.) Say, how ya doin', soldiers?!! *(We hear the sound of soldiers yelling and whistling. Into microphone.)* Can you all hear that back home? Yes, shirts and skirts, Waves and Wacs, civilians and civilettes, we're being broadcast live from somewhere in the Pacific. And we got a great show for ya and a terrific band. *(To Band.)* Fellahs, introduce yourselves. *(The Band Members stand up and introduce themselves — to each other.)* Oh, we're gonna play that way, huh? *(Back to audience.)* All right, we promised you guys a show. Now here's a Joe ya all know. He just

finished shooting his latest motion picture, MGM's new musical, *Over There,* but we got him over here! Buzz Albright!! *(Buzz Albright runs on.)* Help me out, son.

BUZZ. Right with ya.

MC/BUZZ.

IF YOU CAN SING
AND BELIEVE IN ANYTHING
YOU CAN THANK YOUR LUCKY STARS AND STRIPES.

MC. Speak to me, Buzzy. *(Buzz breaks into a short tap solo.)* Buzz Albright! *(Buzz waves and exits.)* Now, I know you fellas are gonna enjoy these girls. You do remember "girls," doncha? Well, here they are! *(Miss South Dakota, Miss North Carolina, Miss Rheingold run on dressed in oversized army, navy, and marine shirts.)* Miss South Dakota —

MISS SOUTH DAKOTA. Yes?

MC. Miss North Carolina —

MISS NORTH CAROLINA. Yes?

MC. Miss Rheingold —

MISS RHEINGOLD. Yeah?

MC. Why doncha show these boys what they're fightin' for?! *(Music in. The Girls sing "PERSONALITY.")*

MISS RHEINGOLD.

WHEN MADAME POMPADOUR WAS ON A BALLROOM FLOOR,
SAID ALL THE GENTLEMEN, "OBVIOUSLY,
THE MADAME HAS THE CUTEST — PERSONALITY."

MISS SOUTH DAKOTA.

AND THINK OF ALL THE BOOKS ABOUT DU BARRY'S LOOKS.
WHAT WAS IT MADE HER THE TOAST OF PAREE?
SHE HAD A WELL DEVELOPED — PERSONALITY.

MISS NORTH CAROLINA.

AND WHAT DID ROMEO SEE IN JULIET,
OR PIERROT IN PIERRETTE,
OR JUPITER IN JUNO?

GIRLS.

YOU KNOW!

(They remove their shirts to reveal red white and blue halters and shorts.)

SO, DON'T YOU YOU SAY I'M SMART
AND HAVE THE KINDEST HEART,
OR WHAT A WONDERFUL SISTER I'D BE.
JUST TELL ME HOW YOU LIKE MY PERSONALITY!

P-E-R-S-O-N-A-L-I-T-Y, YOU SEE!
PERSONALA — PERSONALA — PERSONALITY!

(The Girls wave and go off.)

MC. All right, men, come in for a landing. Now if there's anybody can make you fall in and fly right, it's this Jill. She's been touring the country with Benny Goodman and boys, Benny knows a good thing when he hears it. Let's hear it for Miss Lena George! *(Lena George enters.)* Say, Lena, aren't these guys great?

LENA. Oh, they sure are.

MC. You know, I get all hepped up lookin' at those uniforms. Makes me wanna get out there and be a soldier.

LENA. You'd have to forget all about comfort.

MC. That's for me.

LENA. You'd have to forget all about fear.

MC. That's for me.

LENA. You'd have to forget all about women.

MC. That's for them. *(To "troops.")* Speakin' of women, here's one of the greatest. Show 'em, Lena. *(MC steps back as the band begins the intro to "ALWAYS THE BLUES.")*

LENA. *(To man in the audience.)* How ya doin', soldier? *(Singing.)*

SOLDIER IS LEANING NEXT TO A TREE.
HE'S SAD. HE'S SAD AS CAN BE.
HE LOST A LOVE HE HATED TO LOSE.
YOU SEE, THERE'S ALWAYS THE BLUES.

NERO IS FIDDLIN' OUT ON HIS PORCH
HE'S SAD. HE CARRIES A TORCH.
NOTHING EXCITES HIM NOTHING IS NEWS.
YOU SEE, THERE'S ALWAYS THE BLUES.

COME SUNDAY AND FOLKS FEEL FINE.
THEY'RE HAPPY THAT THEY WERE BORN.
AH, THEN ALONG COMES MONDAY MORNIN'.

ADAM IS LEAVIN' THE GARDEN WITH EVE.
HE'S SAD. 'CAUSE WOULD YOU BELIEVE
HE ATE AN APPLE. THE LORD BLEW A FUSE.
YOU SEE, THERE'S ALWAYS THE BLUES.

COME SUNDAY AND FOLKS FEEL FINE.
THEY'RE HAPPY THAT THEY WERE BORN.
AH, THEN ALONG COMES MONDAY MORNIN'.

YOU'VE GOT A HEARTACHE GETTING YOU DOWN.
YOU'RE SAD. YOU GO PAINTING THE TOWN.
BUT LOOK AT THE PEOPLE LAUGHING IT UP.
WATCH HOW THEY'RE ACTING, HURT AS A PUP.
WELL NEXT TIME AROUND, THEY'LL BE WEARIN' YOUR SHOES.
YOU SEE, THERE'S ALWAYS THE BLUES.

(During the applause, Lena starts out into the house.)

MC. Say, Lena where you goin'? *(Lena returns with Eddie, a young soldier.)*

LENA. I spotted this boy hummin' along during the song. *(À la Mae West.)* I'm a great one for discoverin' talent.

MC. What's your name, soldier?

EDDIE. *(Shy, cornfed.)* Eddie, sir.

MC. Where you from?

EDDIE. Indiana, sir.

LENA. You got a girl, Eddie?

EDDIE. Yes, ma'am. Sure do.

LENA. Do you love her?

EDDIE. Yes, ma'am. Sure do.

MC. How'd you meet her?

EDDIE. Aw, you don't want to hear 'bout that.

LENA/MC. "Sure do."

MC. *(Sets the mike for Eddie.)* This should be about your size, soldier. *(They sit and watch Eddie sing "POLKA DOTS AND MOONBEAMS.")*

EDDIE.

WOULD YOU CARE TO HEAR THE STRANGEST STORY?
AT LEAST IT MAY BE STRANGE TO YOU.
IF YOU SAW IT IN A MOVING PICTURE,
YOU WOULD SAY IT COULDN'T BE TRUE.

A COUNTRY DANCE WAS BEING HELD IN A GARDEN.
I FELT A BUMP AND HEARD AN "OH, BEG YOUR PARDON."
SUDDENLY, I SAW POLKA DOTS AND MOONBEAMS
ALL AROUND A PUG NOSED DREAM.

THE MUSIC STARTED AND WAS I THE PERPLEXED ONE.
I HELD MY BREATH AND SAID, "MAY I HAVE THE NEXT ONE?"
IN MY FRIGHTENED ARMS POLKA DOTS AND MOONBEAMS
SPARKLED ON A PUG NOSED DREAM.

THERE WERE QUESTIONS IN THE EYES OF OTHER DANCERS
AS WE FLOATED OVER THE FLOOR.
THERE WERE QUESTIONS BUT MY HEART KNEW ALL THE
ANSWERS,
AND PERHAPS A FEW THINGS MORE.

NOW IN A COTTAGE BUILT OF LILACS AND LAUGHTER
I KNOW THE MEANING OF THE WORDS "EVER AFTER"
AND I'LL ALWAYS SEE POLKA DOTS AND MOONBEAMS
WHEN I KISS MY PUG NOSED DREAM.

(Eddie notices Buzz and the Girls have drifted out to listen to him. He smiles self-consciously. They encourage him to go on.)

THERE WERE QUESTIONS
BUT MY HEART KNEW ALL THE ANSWERS,
AND PERHAPS A FEW THINGS MORE.

NOW IN A COTTAGE BUILT OF LILAC AND LAUGHTER
I KNOW THE MEANING OF THE WORDS "EVER AFTER"
AND I'LL ALWAYS SEE POLKA DOTS AND MOONBEAMS
WHEN I KISS MY PUG NOSED DREAM.

(During the applause, Eddie starts back into the house. MC motions the Girls to stop him.)

MC. Hey, general, now that we know you can sing, we're not lettin' you off the hook that easy. *(The three Girls sit Eddie down on the side of the stage. To Bandleader.)* How 'bout a little air support, Chuck? *(As the band vamps.)* Now, you boys may not have heard this song out here, but everyone's singin' it back home. Matter of fact, it just won the Academy Award for Johnny Burke and Jimmy Van Heusen. Let's swing it, kids. *(All sing "SWINGING ON A STAR.")*

ALL.

WOULD YOU LIKE TO SWING ON A STAR,
CARRY MOONBEAMS HOME IN A JAR,
AND BE BETTER OFF THAN YOU ARE
OR WOULD YOU RATHER BE A MULE?

MC.

A MULE IS AN ANIMAL WITH LONG FUNNY EARS,

LENA

HE KICKS UP AT ANYTHING HE HEARS.

ALL. Hee-haw!

LENA.

HIS BACK IS BRAWNY
BUT HIS BRAIN IS WEAK,
HE'S JUST PLAIN STUPID
WITH A STUBBORN STREAK.

MC/LENA.

AND, BY THE WAY, IF YOU HATE TO GO TO SCHOOL

ALL.

YOU MAY GROW UP TO BE A MULE.
OR WOULD YOU LIKE TO SWING ON A STAR,
CARRY MOONBEAMS HOME IN A JAR,
AND BE BETTER OFF THAN YOU ARE
OR WOULD YOU RATHER BE A PIG?

BUZZ.

A PIG IS AN ANIMAL WITH DIRT ON HIS FACE,

THE THREE GIRLS.

HIS SHOES ARE A TERRIBLE DISGRACE.
HE'S GOT NO MANNERS WHEN HE EATS HIS FOOD,
HE'S FAT AND LAZY AND EXTREMELY RUDE.

(Buzz, as the "pig," gooses the Girls.)

BUZZ/GIRLS.

BUT IF YOU DON'T CARE A FEATHER OR A FIG

ALL.

YOU MAY GROW UP TO BE A PIG.

(The Girls goose Buzz back.)

BUZZ. *("Threatening.")* Do that again — *(He liked it!)* — one more time!

ALL.

OR WOULD YOU LIKE TO SWING ON A STAR,
CARRY MOONBEAMS HOME IN A JAR
AND BE BETTER OFF THAN YOU ARE
OR WOULD YOU RATHER BE A FISH!

MC. Take it, soldier.

EDDIE.

A FISH WON'T DO ANYTHING BUT SWIM IN A BROOK,
HE CAN'T WRITE HIS NAME OR READ A BOOK.

MC/LENA.

TO FOOL THE PEOPLE IS HIS ONLY THOUGHT

ALL.

AND THOUGH HE'S SLIPPERY, HE STILL GETS CAUGHT.

EDDIE.

BUT THEN IF THAT SORT OF LIFE IS WHAT YOU WISH

ALL.

YOU MAY GROW UP TO BE A FISH!

OR WOULD YOU LIKE TO SWING ON A STAR,
CARRY MOONBEAMS HOME IN A JAR
AND BE BETTER OFF THAN YOU ARE
OR WOULD YOU RATHER BE A —

SWING!
AND SWING!
AND SWING!

SWING, SWING, EVERYBODY'S GOT TO SWING!
SWING, SWING, EVERYBODY'S GOT TO SWING!
SWING, SWING, EVERYBODY'S GOT TO SWING!
SWING, SWING, EVERYBODY'S GOT TO SWING!

DA BA DAP, DA BA DAP, DA BA DA BA;
DA BA DAP, DA BA DAP, DA BA DA BA;
DA BA DAP, DA BA DAP, DA BA DA BA;
DA BA DAP, DA BA DAP, DA BA DA BA;

SWING, SWING, SWING, SWING,
SWING, SWING, SWING, SWING ...

WA, OO-WA, OO-WA, COME ON AND SWING;
WA, OO-WA, OO-WA, COME ON AND SWING;
WA, OO-WA, BA BA BA BA BA BA BOW!

AND ALL THE MONKEYS AREN'T IN THE ZOO.
EV'RY DAY YOU MEET QUITE A FEW.
SO, YOU SEE IT'S ALL UP TO YOU.
YOU CAN BE BETTER THAN YOU ARE
YOU COULD BE SWINGING ON A STAR!

(Suddenly, the PA system crackles on.)

P.A. SYSTEM. Attention, all military personnel. Those men in the 248th Bomber Group, report to the airbase immediately. This is not a drill. On the double, men!

EDDIE. That's me! *(The Band segues into "THANK YOUR LUCKY STARS AND STRIPES" as Eddie goes down the line, hurriedly saying good-bye to the USO cast.)*

ALL. *(Except Eddie.)*

IF YOU LIVE RIGHT,
IF YOU GET TO SLEEP AT NIGHT,
YOU CAN THANK YOUR LUCKY STARS AND STRIPES.

IF YOU FEEL FREE,
IF THERE'S SUGAR IN YOUR TEA,
YOU CAN THANK YOUR LUCKY STARS AND STRIPES.

(Miss North Carolina puts a Hawaiian lei around Eddie's neck. He kisses her, salutes them all, and runs off.)

WOMEN.

THE FOX TROT!

MEN.

THE DIXIE SHAG!

ALL.

AND WHAT'S MORE — THE GRAND OLD FLAG!
IF YOU THINK IT'S WORTH YOUR WHILE
TO SAVE IT — WAVE IT!

IF YOU CAN SING,
AND BELIEVE IN ANYTHING
YOU CAN THANK YOUR LUCKY STARS AND —

(We hear the sound of a plane as it flies overhead. The lei Miss North Carolina put on Eddie falls from the sky! All look up and wave.)

— STRIPES!!

(A huge red, white and blue ribbon drop blankets the stage behind them. And we —)

BLACK OUT

END OF ACT ONE

ACT TWO

Scene 1

Time: 1950 — Evening.

Place: Hotel Roosevelt Ballroom — Akron, Ohio.

As the audience returns from intermission they find themselves in the ballroom of the Hotel Roosevelt, a small hotel in downtown Akron, Ohio. This is the town's only dance spot — a slightly worn version of Roseland.

The Musicians enter wearing white dinner jackets. They take their places and launch into a cha-cha version of "SWINGING ON A STAR."

NOTE: This segment unfolds entirely through song and dance. The actors indicate dialogue without speaking audible lines.

The Coat Check Girl enters with coat hangers on her way to the coat room. The Waiter walks on from the other side carrying a case of soda. Not looking up, they almost bump into each other. They smile awkwardly as the harried Manager enters from the back of the house carrying two coats. He looks disapprovingly at them. The Waiter quickly exits with the soda. The Manager hands the coats to the Coat Check Girl. As she exits into the coat room, the Manager motions out front to the two "customers" that he'll be right back with their stubs. The Coat Check Girl returns, hands the Manager two coat checks and he hurries out front.

A sultry Vocalist enters and walks over to the bandstand. She looks disdainfully down at the stool. The Waiter re-enters with a tray of drinks. She motions him over and gestures to the stool. The Waiter puts down his tray and wipes the top. She moves to sit but he stops her, dusting an imaginary spot on her gown. The Vocalist laughs, sending him off. She sits on the stool and reads her paperback, Peyton Place.

The Waiter serves drinks to the audience members at the tables as the Manager returns. He begins to lecture the Vocalist about reading on the job when the Man and his Date enter. The Man is a regular who loves to show off the latest dance steps. His Date is thrilled to be out with this big spender. The Manager greets them effusively and motions the Coat Check Girl over. She takes their coats. The Man ostentatiously puts a bill in the Bandleader's glass on the piano. The Manager seats the couple.

The Woman Alone appears in the doorway. She hesitates for a moment, takes a breath and enters. This is obviously not her usual stomping grounds.

The Manager approaches her but she indicates she's meeting someone. Nervously, the Woman Alone edges onto the dance floor and looks around. He's not here. She checks her watch then hesitantly asks the Manager for a table.

The Manager motions the Coat Check Girl over. She takes the Woman Alone's wrap. The Manager seats the Woman Alone and exits. The Coat Check Girl returns, hands the Woman Alone her coat check then crosses to hand the Man his.

The Waiter enters with a tray of drinks. As he serves the customers he sings "DON'T LET THAT MOON GET AWAY."

WAITER.

IT'S ONE OF THOSE NIGHTS FOR ADVENTURE,
WE OUGHT TO BE RECKLESSLY GAY.
WHO KNOWS WHAT WE'LL FIND?

(To Coat Check Girl who's busy with the Man.)

SO, IF YOU'RE INCLINED,
DON'T LET THAT MOON GET AWAY.

(The Coat Check Girl turns to look at him. The Waiter quickly goes back to his customers. Embarrassed — did she imagine he was singing to her? — the Coat Check Girl heads back to the Coat Check stool.)

THESE MOMENTS DON'T HAPPEN SO OFTEN;
IT DOESN'T SEEM RIGHT TO DELAY.
IF YOU FEEL IT TOO,
WHATEVER YOU DO
DON'T LET THAT MOON GET AWAY.

AND DON'T LET THIS MEETING ADJOURN,
AND DON'T BE SO READY TO GO;
FOR NOW IS THE RIGHT TIME TO LEARN
WHAT EV'RY YOUNG HEART SHOULD KNOW.

YOUR EYES HAVE A WAY OF REVEALING,
THE THOUGHTS THAT YOU REALLY SHOULD SAY.
IT MAY BE ROMANCE,
SO, WHILE THERE'S A CHANCE,
DON'T LET THAT MOON GET AWAY.

(The Waiter approaches the Woman Alone's table. She mimes two drinks, one for her and her late companion. The Waiter starts off.)

IT MAY BE ROMANCE,

(To Coat Check Girl.)

SO, WHILE THERE'S A CHANCE,

(Back to audience.)

DON'T LET THAT MOON GET AWAY.

(As the Waiter exits he glances at the Man and his Date. The Man is tapping his feet and snapping his fingers furiously to the music, totally ignoring his Date. She sings "ALL YOU WANT TO DO IS DANCE.")

DATE.

THE MUSIC IS PLAYING
A SONG THAT INVITES ROMANCE
BUT YOU, ALL YOU WANT TO DO IS DANCE.

WHILE OTHERS ARE SWAYING
AT LEAST THERE'S A WORD OR GLANCE,
BUT YOU, ALL YOU WANT TO DO IS DANCE.

WHEN YOU HOLD ME LIKE THIS
WHO WOULD NOTICE A KISS?
I KNOW HOW YOUR HEART WOULD BEAT
BUT YOU ONLY CARE ABOUT
THE RHYTHM THAT'S IN YOUR FEET.

THE MUSIC IS PLAYING
A SONG THAT INVITES ROMANCE
AND I, I WANT A CHANCE,
BUT YOU, ALL YOU WANT TO DO IS DANCE.
ALL YOU WANT TO DO IS DANCE.
ALL YOU WANT TO DO IS DANCE.

(The music segues into "YOU DANCED WITH DYNAMITE." The Man grabs his Date and energetically tries a Fred and Ginger routine which has her inadvertently twirled into walls and dropped onto the floor.)

MAN.

YOU DIDN'T KNOW TONIGHT
YOU DANCED WITH DYNAMITE.
SUPPOSE YOUR EYES HAD FLASHED WITH FLAME
AND THOUGH I WOULD HAVE BEEN THE BLAME,
YOU DANCED WITH DYNAMITE JUST THE SAME.

YOU HAD A LOT OF FEAR.
YOUR LIPS WERE MUCH TO NEAR
AND WHAT YOU THOUGHT WAS JUST A LARK,
IT NEEDED JUST A TINY SPARK
YOU DANCED WITH DYNAMITE IN THE DARK.

THE FLOOR BEGAN TO SWAY
AND STRANGE TO SAY
THE CEILING WHIRLED ABOUT.

WE PASSED BY PARADISE
AND ONCE OR TWICE
I NEARLY CRIED, "LOOK OUT!"

(He spins her out, sending her crashing into the wall.)

AND WHILE WE'RE HERE ALONE
YOU'RE IN A DANGER ZONE
AND DO YOU DARE TO LINGER YET.
TO LIGHT ANOTHER CIGARETTE
YOU DANCED WITH DYNAMITE DON'T FORGET.

DATE.

ALL YOU WANT TO DO IS DANCE.

MAN.

YOU DANCED WITH DYNAMITE.

DATE.

ALL YOU WANT TO DO IS DANCE.

MAN.

YOU DANCED WITH DYNAMITE.

DATE.

ALL YOU WANT TO DO IS DANCE ... DANCE!

MAN.

YOU DANCED WITH DYNAMITE!

(The number becomes a wrestling match, ending with the Date pinning him to the floor. During the applause, she hurries back to the table. The Man crawls after her. The Waiter almost trips over him as he enters. Embarrassed, the Man pretends to be looking for a contact lens. The Waiter continues to the Woman Alone's table and sets down the two drinks she ordered. Embarrassed, she gestures for him to take the other back. Her date isn't coming, she's been stood up. She takes a sip of her drink, trying not to feel so foolish and alone. The Manager enters and motions the Vocalist it's time for her number. The Vocalist steps up to the microphone and sings "IMAGINATION.")

VOCALIST.

IMAGINATION IS FUNNY,
IT MAKES A CLOUDY DAY SUNNY,
MAKES A BEE THINK OF HONEY,
JUST AS I THINK OF YOU

IMAGINATION IS CRAZY,
YOUR WHOLE PERSPECTIVE GETS HAZY,
STARTS YOU ASKING A DAISY,
WHAT TO DO — WHAT TO DO?

HAVE YOU EVER FELT A GENTLE TOUCH
AND THEN A KISS AND THEN AND THEN
FIND IT'S ONLY YOUR IMAGINATION AGAIN?

OH, WELL.

IMAGINATION IS SILLY,
YOU GO AROUND WILLY NILLY.
FOR EXAMPLE, I GO AROUND WANTING YOU
AND YET, I CAN'T IMAGINE THAT YOU WANT ME, TOO.

(The Waiter and the Coat Check Girl drift onto the floor, watching the "couples" dancing out front. The Waiter's white towel falls from his shoulder. They bend down to pick it up and accidentally touch hands. The others freeze and the lights change as time stands still. The Waiter and the Coat Check Girl let their own imaginations soar and their inner feelings show. The two enact a fantasy romance through a pas de deux. At the end, they find themselves where they started, both bending down to pick up the towel. The lights change. Time moves on. She walks back to her post; he to his.)

HAVE YOU EVER FELT A GENTLE TOUCH
AND THEN A KISS AND THEN AND THEN

FIND IT'S ONLY YOUR IMAGINATION AGAIN?
OH, WELL.

IMAGINATION IS SILLY,
YOU GO AROUND WILLY NILLY.
FOR EXAMPLE, I GO AROUND WANTING YOU
AND YET, I CAN'T IMAGINE THAT YOU WANT ME, TOO.

(The Vocalist bows to the applause and exits. The Man and his Date are ready to leave. The Coat Check Girl gets their coats. As the Manager escorts the couple out, he notices the Waiter and the Coat Check Girl staring at one another. He snaps his fingers — get back to work. The Waiter smiles at the Coat Check Girl and exits. The Woman Alone, who has watched it all, beckons the Coat Check Girl over. She sings "IT COULD HAPPEN TO YOU.")

WOMAN ALONE.

DO YOU BELIEVE IN CHARMS AND SPELLS,
IN MYSTIC WORDS AND MAGIC WANDS AND WISHING WELLS?
DON'T LOOK SO WISE. DON'T SHOW YOUR SCORN,
WATCH YOURSELF, I WARN YOU.

HIDE YOUR HEART FROM SIGHT,
LOCK YOUR DREAMS AT NIGHT,
IT COULD HAPPEN TO YOU.

DON'T COUNT STARS
OR YOU MIGHT STUMBLE.
SOMEONE DROPS A SIGH
AND DOWN YOU TUMBLE.

KEEP AN EYE ON SPRING.
RUN WHEN CHURCH BELLS RING.
IT COULD HAPPEN TO YOU.

ALL I DID WAS WONDER
HOW HIS ARMS WOULD BE,
AND IT HAPPENED TO ME!

(The Coat Check Girl steals a glance toward where the Waiter exited. The Woman Alone smiles sadly, knowing her words go unheeded. She hands the Coat Check Girl her coat check. The Coat Check Girl exits into the coat room. To herself.)

DON'T COUNT STARS
OR YOU MIGHT STUMBLE.
SOMEONE DROPS A SIGH
AND DOWN YOU TUMBLE.

(The Coat Check Girl comes back with the Woman Alone's coat. To Coat Check Girl.)

KEEP AN EYE ON SPRING.
RUN WHEN CHURCH BELLS RING.
IT COULD HAPPEN TO YOU.

ALL I DID WAS WONDER
HOW HIS ARMS WOULD BE,
AND IT HAPPENED TO ME!

(The Woman Alone leaves as she came — alone. The lights start to dim. The dance floor is deserted. The Waiter enters. He and the Coat Check Girl look at each other and race into each other's arms. He lifts her high above him and they spin delightedly to the last strains of "IMAGINATION" ... as the lights ... fade to black.)

Transition to Scene 2*

On a movie screen appears a montage of clips from the "Road To" movies, starring Bing Crosby, Bob Hope and Dorothy Lamour, songs written by Johnny Burke and Jimmy Van Heusen. The montage ends with shots from the trailer to Road To Morocco *and the legend:* "Yes, It's Bing! It's Bob! It's Dorothy! Hitting the Road again!! *The lights fade up as we segue to ...*

* See Author's Note in back of book.

Scene 2

Time: 1951.

Place: Paramount Sound Studios.

The screen becomes a Moroccan desert as Bing and Bob ride on stage, sitting atop a camel.

BING/BOB.

WE'RE OFF ON THE ROAD TO MOROCCO
THIS TAXI IS TOUGH ON THE SPINE.

BOB. Should've taken the bus.

BING. Oh, cabby!

BOB.

WHERE WE'RE GOIN',

BING.

WHY WE'RE GOIN',

BING/BOB.

HOW CAN WE BE SURE?

BING.

I'LL LAY YOU 8 TO 5 THAT WE MEET DOROTHY LAMOUR.

BOB. Look out! *(They get off the camel which tracks offstage.)*

BING/BOB.

WE'RE OFF ON THE ROAD TO MOROCCO

BING. To live the simple life.

BING/BOB.

A TENT WITH A VIEW WILL DO FINE.

BOB. Not too near the sand.

BING/BOB.

THE FUNNY STREETS ARE NICE AND DARK,
THE MUSIC IS UNIQUE.
PERHAPS WE'LL MEET A KIDNAPPED GIRL
AND I'LL BECOME HER SHEIK.
"Tres chic!"
WE CERTAINLY DO GET AROUND
LIKE WEBSTER'S DICTIONARY WE'RE MOROCCO BOUND!

(Dorothy runs on, dressed as a Moroccan Princess.)

DOROTHY. Help! Help!

BING. Looks like a damsel in distress.

BOB. Dis dress, dat dress. She'd look good in anything!

DOROTHY. *(To the boys.)* Quick, hide me! *(She hides behind them as the Sheik stalks on. He looks around, glares suspiciously at Bing and Bob, and stalks off. To the boys.)* Thank you. I'll see you are handsomely rewarded.

BOB. Don't be silly. A simple kiss on the cheek and twenty-four hours alone in a tent will do.

BING. Down, boy. So, who was that ruffian?

DOROTHY. The Sheik of Pakistan. I'm the Princess of Morocco and I've been pledged to marry him tomorrow. But I want to marry for love not money.

BOB. Then I'm your boy. I'm broke.

BING. Kid loves to brag.

DOROTHY. Please, you must help me get away.

BING. Well, sure. Where did you want to go?

DOROTHY. Home.

BOB. Am I missing a plot point? You're the Princess of Morocco.

DOROTHY. I am.

BING. And this is Morocco.

DOROTHY. It is.

BING/BOB. *(Embracing her.)* Welcome home, Princess.

DOROTHY. *(Pushes them away.)* You don't understand. This isn't my home. You see — *(She steps forward. The lights change. "Melodrama music." Emoting.)* When I was a young girl, I was kidnapped from my home and sold into a slave cartel where I was finally bought by the King of Morocco who wanted a virgin for his next wife but when he saw how young I was he took pity on me and raised me as his daughter instead. *(She steps back. The lights restore.)*

BOB. *(To audience.)* That's got more holes than my sock.

BING. So, where's home?

DOROTHY. *(Rhapsodic.)* Florida.

BING/BOB. Florida?!

DOROTHY. You know, Miami Beach, Fort Lauderdale. Oh, please, won't you help me return to my homeland?

BING. *(Snuggling up.)* Well, I've always been a sucker for a beautiful woman.

BOB. *(Taps her shoulder.)* Did I mention I'm broke?

DOROTHY. Oh, thank you. But how will we get there? *(A car rolls on as the Band plays the intro to "APALACHICOLA, FLA.")*

BOB. Is that a mirage?

BING. No, I think it's a Chrysler. *(They get into the car; Bing behind the wheel, Dorothy in the middle.)*

BING/BOB/DOROTHY.

WE'RE FULL OF GLEE,
MY BUDDIES AND ME.
NO LONGER WILL WE ROAM.

DON'T GET US WRONG.
THIS AIN'T JUST A SONG.
WE REALLY ARE GOING HOME.

(Behind them we see a moving country road on the screen.)

WE'RE ON OUR WAY TO APALACHICOLA, FLA
MAGNOLIA TREES IN BLOSSOM AND A PRETTY SOUTHERN GAL,
IT'S BETTER THAN THE ORANGE GROVES IN CUCUMONGA, CAL.

(The screen cuts to a rainy, stormy road as, out of camera range, a Grip wearing coveralls with the Paramount logo, stands on a ladder and spritzes water at them. Dorothy holds up an umbrella as the boys wave windshield wipers.)

WE'RE GONNA STAY ALONG THE APALACHICOLA BAY.

(The screen cuts to a snowy road. The Grip now tosses "snowflakes" over their heads.)

WE MAY STOP AT OCHLACKONEE FOR SOME HOMINY GRITS
OR PASS THROUGH TALLAHASSEE IF THE WEATHER PERMITS.

(The screen changes back to the country road. The Grip exits.)

BUT, WE'RE ON OUR WAY TO APALACHICOLA,

(They plop on sunglasses.)

F — L — A!

(The music falters to a stop as the country road slows down and then freezes on screen.)

DOROTHY. Why did we stop?

BING. Looks like we're out of gas, Princess. *(Gets out.)* There's gotta be a gas station somewhere.

BOB. *(Puts his arm around Dorothy.)* You go look. I'll mind the store.

DOROTHY. *(Gets out of the car.)* There must be another way to travel.

BING. Well, we could take a plane. *(Takes bills out of his pocket.)* I've got twenty. Junior?

BOB. *(Takes bills out of his pocket.)* I've got fifty.

DOROTHY. I thought you were broke.

BOB. Spiritually.

BING. Together this would only buy us two tickets. *(Beat. The guys look at each other.)*

BING/BOB. *(The old choosing game.)* Rock, paper, scissor —

DOROTHY. Quick! Hide me! *(The Sheik appears. Dorothy hides behind the boys. The Sheik looks around, glares at Bing and Bob and stalks off. Dorothy surreptitiously takes the money out of the boys' hands and runs off the other way.)*

BING. *(Turning around.)* Well, Princess — Say, where'd she go?

BOB. I don't know.

BING. Where's our money?

BOB. I don't know.

BING. What's my next line?

BOB. I don't know. *(Music in — a conga beat. The car rolls off as a banana tree rolls on. The road on screen becomes a rippling Brazilian Beach and two Girls samba on in Carmen Miranda outfits.)*

BING. Say, where are we?

BOB. *(Admiring the Girls.)* I don't know, but I like the scenery. *(Bing and Bob grab sombreros off the tree and samba toward the Girls. They bump into each other.)*

BING. This picture isn't big enough for both of us.

BOB. *(Heading for the Girls.)* I'll miss ya. *(Bing pulls him back. They sing "YOU DON'T HAVE TO KNOW THE LANGUAGE.")*

BING/BOB.

SUPPOSING YOU NEED A VACATION?
BRAZIL IS THE PLACE YOU SHOULD BE.

GIRLS. *(Eyeing the guys.) Muy guapo!*

BING/BOB.

SO, YOU CAN'T UNDERSTAND WHAT THEY'RE SAYING.
YOU CAN'T READ A SIGN THAT YOU SEE,

BING/BOB/GIRLS.

BUT, YOU DON'T HAVE TO KNOW THE LANGUAGE
WITH A MOON IN THE SKY AND A GIRL IN YOUR ARMS
AND A LOOK IN HER EYE.

(Dorothy enters, disguised in a Carmen Miranda outfit with a <u>*huge*</u> *fruit basket on her head. Unseen by Bing, Bob and the Girls, she staggers across the stage, barely able to move under the weight.)*

BING/BOB.

WHEN SHE SMILES YOUR WAY —

(The Sheik stalks on, looking for her. Dorothy poses as one of the girls.)

GIRLS.

WHAT MORE WOULD YOU WANT ANYONE TO SAY!

(The Sheik tramps off past her.)

BING/BOB.

SO, YOU SIGH, JUST SIGH.

(As Dorothy cranes her neck to see if he's gone, the weight of her headdress sends her careening backwards.)

BING/BOB/GIRLS.

YOU DON'T HAVE TO MENTION THAT YANKEE PHRASE,
"AY, AY."

(Bing and Bob and the girls form a conga line. Dorothy desperately grabs on to the back of the line to steady herself.)

PERHAPS WHEN YOU END YOUR VACATION,

(The Sheik returns. As he stealthily inches across the stage, the first Girl grabs his behind, making him the head of the conga line.)

YOU'LL BRING BACK A BIT OF BRAZIL.

(Bing, Bob and the Girls dance to the sides. Caught up in the rhythm, Dorothy and the Sheik samba around each other, unaware who their partner is.)

SO, YOU CAN'T UNDERSTAND WHAT SHE'S SAYING.

(Dorothy realizes it's the Sheik! She shakes her head, causing two bananas to dangle from the headdress, and holds her arms out — a make-shift banana tree!)

YOU NEED AN INTERPRETER STILL,

(The Sheik notices the tree. Hungry, he pulls off one of the bananas — and sees her face. Dorothy runs off, the Sheik in hot pursuit.)

BUT YOU DON'T HAVE TO KNOW THE LANGUAGE
WITH A MOON IN THE SKY AND A GIRL IN YOUR ARMS
AND A LOOK IN HER EYE.

NO, YOU DON'T HAVE TO KNOW THE LANGUAGE
IF YOU DON'T WANT TO SAY GOOD — BYE.

(The Girls start to samba off with Bob.)

BING. Hey, what about me?!

BOB. No speakee Englee, señor. *(He exits with the Girls.)*

BING. *(Mutters.)* I'm supposed to get the girl. It's in my contract. *(Sighs.)* What am I going to do now? *(As the banana tree rolls past him, he hangs his sombrero on it and takes a fedora and raincoat off of the back. A tree stump rolls on from the other side, arriving underneath him just as he sits. On the screen, clouds flow gently by as Bing sings "GOING MY WAY.")*

THIS ROAD LEADS TO RAINBOWVILLE.
GOING MY WAY?
UP AHEAD IS BLUEBIRD HILL.
GOING MY WAY?

JUST PACK A BASKET FULL OF WISHES
AND OFF YOU START
WITH SUNDAY MORNING IN YOUR HEART.

'ROUND THE BEND YOU'LL SEE A SIGN,
"DREAMER'S HIGHWAY."
HAPPINESS IS DOWN THE LINE.
GOING MY WAY?

THE SMILES YOU'LL GATHER
WILL LOOK WELL ON YOU.
OH, I HOPE YOU'RE GOING MY WAY, TOO.

(Bob pushes his own tree stump on stage.)

BOB. *(To audience.)* My stump's not in the union. *(To Bing.)* How come you get a solo?

BING. Top billing, boy. Where are the girls?

BOB. They left.

BING. Tough luck.

BOB. Tough girls. *(Dorothy runs on, now wearing a sarong.)*

DOROTHY. Help! Help!

BING. *(To Bob.)* Could be a flashback.

DOROTHY. Quick! Hide me! *(Dorothy hides behind the guys as the Sheik stalks on, glares yet again at the boys, and exits.)* Oh, thank you.

BING. Ixnay on the gratitude, girlie.

BOB. You stole our money.

DOROTHY. But I can explain. You see — *(She steps forward. The lights change. "Melodrama music." Emoting.)* You could only afford two tickets and I didn't want to break up such a strong friendship so I tried to see if I could rent a small plane to take us all back to America but all the airports were closed for the Xaviar Cugat Festival and then the Sheik showed up and I've been running ever since. *(She steps back. The lights restore. To Bob.)* You do believe me?

BOB. Believe you! I don't believe — *(Dorothy kisses him.)* I believe. I believe.

BING. *(Turns Dorothy to him.)* Now that you've tasted the h'ors d'ouerve. *(He moves to kiss her. Bob does the same.)*

BOB. Hands off, smart boy. She's mine.

BING. Yeah?

BOB. *(Spoiling for a fight.)* Yeah.

BING. *(Takes a step in.)* Yeah?!

BOB. *(Nose to nose.)* Yeah!!

BING. *(Makes a fist.)* There's only one way to settle this.

BOB. *(Makes a fist.)* Okay by me. *(Beat.)*

BING/BOB. *(Choosing again.)* Rock, paper, scissor —

DOROTHY. Boys, could you hurry up? This sarong is awfully tight.

BING/BOB. What's "sarong" with that?

DOROTHY. There must be another way to travel. Won't you help me? I'm so anxious to get home to my family, and the orange groves, and the smell of jasmine in the air. *(Sits on a tree stump, her feet on the other.)* I remember it all so vividly. *(Music in as the Grip pushes on a dock carrying the Southern Woman, fanning herself languidly.)*

BOB. What's she doing here?

BING. *(Pushing Dorothy off stage.)* Atmosphere. C'mon, Junior.

BOB. *(Mutters as he follows.)* He gets a solo. She gets a solo. What am I, chopped liver? *(A river fades up on the screen as the Southern Woman sings "SHADOWS ON THE SWANEE.")*

SOUTHERN WOMAN.

SHADOWS ON THE SWANEE,

(She notices the Grip still standing there. Annoyed, she waves him off. It's her number.)

IN THE EVENING BY THE MOONLIGHT,
LOVERS EV'RYWHERE;
HOW I WISH THAT I WERE THERE.

(Bing, Bob and Dorothy appear with a "canoe" attached to their waists between them. They "paddle" center, providing vocal back-up for the Southern Woman.)

SOUTHERN WOMAN/BING/BOB/DOROTHY.

WHY DID I WANDER SO FAR AWAY,
FROM ALL MY SWEET-HEART SCENES?
NEVER THOUGHT THAT I'D BE LONESOME,
BUT NOW I KNOW JUST WHAT IT MEANS,

LONGIN',

BING. *(His trademark scatting.)* Buh, buh, buh, buh, buh, buh, boo.

SOUTHERN WOMAN.

HOW I'M LONGIN',

BOB. *(Trying it.)* Buh, buh, buh, buh — *(Dorothy hits Bob with her parasol. He stops.)*

SOUTHERN WOMAN.

TO BE WALKIN' WITH MY SWEETIE,
THEN THERE'D BE TWO MORE,

(The dock begins to roll offstage. The three paddle after it.)

SOUTHERN WOMAN/BING/BOB/DOROTHY.

SHADOWS ON THE SWANEE —

(Just as the canoe reaches the wings, the Sheik appears and grabs Dorothy out of the boat. Unaware, the boys continue off.)

DOROTHY. Help! Help! Boys, help! *(The screen becomes a map of the United States with two sets of footprints running from state to state. The Sheik claps his hands and the two Girls enter, now dressed as Pakistani women in long black robes and veils. They hold a large, colorful tapestry between them. The Sheik orders Dorothy behind the tapestry. On the screen, the map dissolves to a Moorish Palace as the Sheik sings "PAKISTAN.")*

SHEIK.

I'M GONNA PACK YOU OFF TO PAKISTAN.
YOU'RE GONNA COOL ME WITH A BAMBOO FAN.
YOU'RE GONNA FEED ME GRAPES AND SERVE ME TEA.

DOROTHY. *(Sticking her head out.)*

SOME OTHER GIRL NOT ME!

GIRLS. *(High wails.)*

AIIIIIIIIIIIIIIIIIIIIIII!
AIIIIIIIIIIIIIIIIIIIIIII!

(The Girls provide back-up.)

SHEIK.

I'M GONNA PACK YOU OFF TO PAKISTAN.
WE'RE GONNA HOP AN EAST BOUND CARAVAN.
YOU'RE GONNA LEARN TO CHARM A SNAKE OR TWO.

GIRLS.

AND DANCE THE HOOCHIE-COO!

SHEIK.

THERE'LL BE NO MORE CHASING YOU THROUGH THE SAND.
YOU CAN JOIN MY HUNDRED OTHER SWEETHEARTS,
WHILE I RULE THE LAND.

SO DON'T GIVE ME A DISAPPOINTED LOOK.
YOU MUST LEARN TO CLEAN AND LEARN TO COOK.
YOU MUST BE A WIFE WHO SERVES HER MAN.
WE'RE PACKIN' OFF TO PAKISTAN!

(He claps his hands again and the Girls move off revealing Dorothy in her Princess garb, but now with a wedding veil and bridal bouquet. The Sheik nods his approval.)

GIRLS. *(As they exit.)*

AIIIIIIIIIIIIIIIIIIIIIII!

AIIIIIIIIIIIIIIIIIIIIIII!

(The Sheik doesn't notice that as the Girls reach the wings they are suddenly replaced by Bing and Bob, also dressed as Pakistani women in long black robes and veils. Holding the tapestry, the boys undulate back on, singing in the same high pitched, whiny voices as the Girls were.)

BING/BOB.

AIIIIIIIIIIIIIIIIIIIIII!

AIIIIIIIIIIIIIIIIIIIIII!

HE'S GONNA PACK YOU OFF TO PAKISTAN.

YOU'RE GONNA COOL HIM WITH A BAMBOO FAN.

YOU'RE GONNA FEED HIM GRAPES AND SERVE HIM TEA.

(Bob covertly pulls down his veil to show Dorothy who they are. Dorothy, with rescue at hand, feigns compliance to the Sheik.)

DOROTHY/SHEIK.

A MODEL WIFE I'LL/YOU'LL BE.

(The boys lay the tapestry down. Dorothy cajoles the Sheik onto it.)

THERE'LL BE NO MORE CHASING ME/YOU THROUGH THE SAND.

DOROTHY.

I WILL JOIN YOUR HUNDRED OTHER SWEETHEARTS,

SHEIK.

WHILE I RULE THE LAND.

DOROTHY.

I WILL LEARN TO CLEAN AND LEARN TO COOK.

SHEIK

YOU WILL BE A WIFE WHO SERVES A —

BOB.

SHNOOK!

(The Sheik glowers at Bob. Dorothy quickly turns him back to her.)

DOROTHY.

I WILL BE A WIFE WHO SERVES HER MAN.

(She pops him one in the jaw. The Sheik crumples onto the tapestry.)

BING/BOB/DOROTHY.

LET'S PACK HIM OFF TO PAKISTAN!

(The three gleefully sing as they wrap the Sheik in the tapestry.)

AIIIIIIIIIIIIIIIIIIIII!

AIIIIIIIIIIIIIIIIIIIII!

AIIIIIIIIIIIIIIIIIIIII!

(They clap their hands. The Grip enters and drags the Sheik off. A three-way handshake.)

WE PACKED HIM OFF TO PAKISTAN!

DOROTHY. You were terrific.

BING. *(As he and Bob remove their robes.)* So, what's the plan, Princess? On to Florida?

DOROTHY. Actually, I'd like to go home.

BOB. Yeah, Florida.

DOROTHY. No, you see — *(She steps forward. The lights change. "Melodrama Music." Emoting.)* I realize now that home is where the heart is. And my heart is back in Morocco. *(Her voice begins to change — younger, lighter.)* So if I ever go looking for my heart's desire again, I won't look any further than my own backyard. Because if it isn't there, I never really lost it to begin with. *(To Bing and Bob.)* Why this has all been like a dream. And you were there. And you were there. Oh, Auntie Em —

BING. Whoa, sister. Wrong Dorothy. *(The lights restore.)*

DOROTHY. *(Herself again.)* Please, won't you take me back.

BING. Well, it's a long road.

BOB. *(Limbering up his thumb to hitchhike.)* Better warm up the digit.

BING. I've got a better idea. *(He whistles and the camel rolls on. Music in — "ROAD TO MOROCCO REPRISE.")*

BOB. Here we go again!

BING/BOB/DOROTHY.

WE'RE OFF ON THE ROAD TO MOROCCO.

DOROTHY.

AND I KNOW HOW WE'LL PASS THE TIME.

BING. Tell it to me, sweetly.

DOROTHY. *(To Bing.)*

I'LL WHISPER HOW I LOVE YOU
TO THE STRAINS OF NATIVE FLUTES,

(To Bob.)

AND YOUR ARMS WILL THRILL ME MORE
THAN ALL THE CHUTE-THE-CHUTES.

BING/BOB/DOROTHY.

WE'RE OFF ON THE ROAD TO MOROCCO,
SO LET'S DREAM FOR THE PRICE OF A DIME.

WE'LL RIDE A MAGIC CARPET
THAT LOOKS ABSOLUTELY REAL.
DON'T YOU THINK THAT'S MORE ROMANTIC
THAN THE FERRIS WHEEL?

WE CERTAINLY DO GET AROUND.
LIKE WEBSTER'S DICTIONARY —

(Bing and Dorothy hop on the camel.)

BOB. — or a complete set of Shakespeare that you buy in a corner drugstore for a dollar ninety-eight! *(Bob grabs the reins and leads the camel off.)*

BING/BOB/DOROTHY. *(Waving.)*

— WE'RE MOROCCO BOUND!

(The screen cuts to a speaking camel!)

CAMEL. *(Bob's voice.)* Well, there they go again! *(And, then, Paramount's signature logo of ... "The End.")* *

BLACKOUT

Transition to Scene 3*

We hear the simple strains of "PENNIES FROM HEAVEN." On the screen appears a collage of sheet music and records of some of Johnny Burke's biggest hits. Interspersed will be photographs of the following stars as they speak about Johnny.

LENA HORNE. *(V.O.)* Johnny Burke had a nickname. He was called "The Poet." And that's why I loved his lyrics. They were literate, beautiful and poetic. I especially liked recording "But, Beautiful," because of his phrasing and his use of beautiful words. Every singer wants that.

JOHNNY MATHIS. *(V.O.)* When I was about thirteen years old, years ago, I used to sing at a local jazz club in San Francisco. And I met one of the great geniuses of all time, Erroll Garner. Every night he would play this song he wrote. There were no words, just this wonderful melody. And I told him — as only a kid of thirteen could tell a great performer like Erroll Garner — that one day I would record his song. Years later I heard it again, only now it had the most

* See Author's Note in back of book.

beautiful haunting lyric I could imagine. Of course, the first chance I had to do an album, I recorded it. And that song was "Misty."

DORIS DAY. *(V.O.)* I started out as a band singer when I was sixteen, way before I ever thought about acting in movies. But even then, instinctively I guess, I approached a song as an actress, which is why I've always loved Johnny Burke. It was so easy to feel the emotion in his lyrics, and his songs always told a story in such an interesting way. You know, it's fitting he wrote a song called "Imagination." If ever a man had imagination — it was Johnny Burke.

TONY BENNETT. *(V.O.)* I'm a storyteller. So, you know, if you're singing a song like "Here's That Rainy Day," it's tremendous because it tells a story. It holds the audience. Every great musician that I respect, the best ones considered Jimmy Van Heusen and Johnny Burke their favorite. I never met Johnny Burke but I made a recording of "Oh You Crazy Moon," and I was very pleased with the sound of it. And I walked out thinking what a nice song this is and someone told me Johnny Burke just died. The same moment that I recorded the song was the same moment that he died. It was just one of those strange coincidences.

LENA HORNE. *(V.O.)* And now, ladies and gentlemen, the timeless songs of "The Poet" — Johnny Burke. *(The screen flies out to reveal ...)*

Scene 3

Time: The Present — Evening.

Place: The Starlight Supper Club — Manhattan.

A glistening rooftop supper club, set against the backdrop of a beautiful Manhattan skyline at night.

Woman 3 sits on the baby grand. She sings "BUT, BEAUTIFUL."

WOMAN 3.

WHO CAN SAY WHAT LOVE IS?
DOES IT START IN THE MIND OR THE HEART?
WHEN I HEAR DISCUSSIONS ON WHAT LOVE IS
EVERYBODY SPEAKS A DIFFERENT PART.

LOVE IS FUNNY OR IT'S SAD
OR IT'S QUIET OR IT'S MAD:

IT'S A GOOD THING OR IT'S BAD,
BUT BEAUTIFUL!

(Man 1 walks on.)

BEAUTIFUL TO TAKE A CHANCE
AND IF YOU FALL, YOU FALL.

(Woman 1 enters. She and Man 1 share a look, obviously attracted. Encouraging them.)

AND YOU'RE THINKING ...

WOMAN 3/WOMAN 1/MAN 1.

I WOULDN'T MIND AT ALL.

(Man 1 and Woman 1 sing "LIKE SOMEONE IN LOVE" and "MOONLIGHT BECOMES YOU.")

WOMAN 1.

LATELY, I FIND MYSELF OUT GAZING AT STARS,
HEARING GUITARS, LIKE SOMEONE IN LOVE.
SOMETIMES THE THINGS I DO ASTOUND ME,
MOSTLY WHENEVER YOU'RE AROUND ME.

(Man 1 walks toward her.)

MAN 1.

MOONLIGHT BECOMES YOU,
IT GOES WITH YOUR HAIR,
YOU CERTAINLY KNOW THE RIGHT THING TO WEAR.

MOONLIGHT BECOMES YOU,
I'M THRILLED AT THE SIGHT,
AND I COULD GET SO ROMANTIC TONIGHT.

YOU'RE ALL DRESSED UP TO GO DREAMING,
NOW DON'T TELL ME I'M WRONG.
AND WHAT A NIGHT TO GO DREAMING,
MIND IF I TAG ALONG?

IF I SAY I LOVE YOU,
I WANT YOU TO KNOW
IT'S NOT JUST BECAUSE
THERE'S MOONLIGHT ALTHOUGH —
MOONLIGHT BECOMES YOU SO.

(As Man 1 and Woman 1 move to the side of the stage Man 2 enters. He watches them.)

WOMAN 3. *(Softly.)*

LOVE IS TEARFUL OR IT'S GAY.
IT'S A PROBLEM OR IT'S PLAY.

WOMAN 3/MAN 2.

IT'S A HEARTACHE EITHER WAY ...

(Man 2 sings "IF LOVE AIN'T THERE [IT AIN'T THERE].")

MAN 2.

YOU CAN PRAISE HER EYES AND ADORE HER HAIR,
BUT IF LOVE AIN'T THERE, IT AIN'T THERE.
AND YOU CAN WALK HER HOME IN THE WARM SPRING AIR,
BUT IF LOVE AIN'T THERE, IT AIN'T THERE.
NO, IF LOVE AIN'T THERE ... IT AIN'T THERE.

(As he starts off-stage Woman 2 enters, catching his eye. She smiles flirtatiously and sings "SUNDAY, MONDAY OR ALWAYS.")

WOMAN 2.

WON'T YOU TELL ME WHEN
WE WILL MEET AGAIN,
SUNDAY, MONDAY OR ALWAYS?

IF YOU'RE SATISFIED,
I'LL BE AT YOUR SIDE,
SUNDAY, MONDAY, OR ALWAYS.

NO NEED TO TELL ME NOW
WHAT MAKES THE WORLD GO 'ROUND,
WHEN AT THE SIGHT OF YOU
MY HEART BEGINS TO POUND AND POUND,

AND WHAT AM I TO DO?
CAN'T I BE WITH YOU,
SUNDAY, MONDAY OR ALWAYS?

(Man 2 begins to walk away. Woman 2 follows, scatting seductively. He stops. This woman's impossible to resist.)

NO NEED TO TELL ME NOW
WHAT MAKES THE WORLD GO 'ROUND,
WHEN AT THE SIGHT OF YOU
MY HEART BEGINS TO POUND AND POUND ...

(Now it's her turn. Teasing, she backs away. Smitten, Man 2 follows.)

AND WHAT AM I TO DO?
CAN'T I BE WITH YOU,
SUNDAY, MONDAY —
TUESDAY, WEDNESDAY, THURSDAY, FRIDAY —
ANY DAY OF THE WEEK!

SUNDAY, MONDAY, OR ALWAYS!

(Man 2 and Woman 2 walk to the other side of the stage. Woman 3 looks wistfully at both couples.)

WOMAN 3.

THAT WOULD BE BUT BEAUTIFUL,
THAT WOULD BE BUT BEAUTIFUL,
THAT WOULD BE BUT BEAUTIFUL,
I KNOW.

(She gets off the piano and starts to exit as Man 3 enters from the other side.)

MAN 3. *(Softly.)* Look ... *(She stops and turns to face him. Man 3 sings "MISTY.")*

LOOK ... AT ME,
I'M AS HELPLESS AS A KITTEN UP A TREE
AND I FEEL LIKE I'M CLINGING TO A CLOUD.
I CAN'T UNDERSTAND,
I GET MISTY JUST HOLDING YOUR HAND.

WALK MY WAY
AND A THOUSAND VIOLINS BEGAN TO PLAY,
OR IT MIGHT BE THE SOUND OF YOUR HELLO.
THAT MUSIC I HEAR,
I GET MISTY, THE MOMENT YOU'RE NEAR.

YOU CAN SAY THAT YOU'RE LEADING ME ON,
BUT IT'S JUST WHAT I WANT YOU TO DO.
DON'T YOU NOTICE HOW HOPELESSLY I'M LOST?
THAT'S WHY I'M FOLLOWING YOU.

ON MY OWN,
WOULD I WANDER THROUGH THIS WONDERLAND ALONE,
NEVER KNOWING MY RIGHT FOOT FROM MY LEFT,
MY HAT FROM MY GLOVE,
I'M TOO MISTY AND TOO MUCH IN LOVE.
I'M TOO MISTY AND TOO MUCH IN LOVE.

(Our three couples are so involved with each other, they don't see ... Woman 4 — standing away from the others. She sings "HERE'S THAT RAINY DAY.")

WOMAN 4.

MAYBE I SHOULD HAVE SAVED
THOSE LEFT OVER DREAMS;
FUNNY BUT HERE'S THAT RAINY DAY.

HERE'S THAT RAINY DAY THEY TOLD ME ABOUT,
AND I LAUGHED AT THE THOUGHT
THAT IT MIGHT TURN OUT THIS WAY.

WHERE IS THAT WORN OUT WISH
THAT I THREW ASIDE,
AFTER IT BROUGHT MY LOVER NEAR?
FUNNY HOW LOVE BECOMES
A COLD RAINY DAY.
FUNNY THAT RAINY DAY IS HERE.

(Man 1 turns to her.)

MAN 1. *(Gently.)*

EVERY TIME IT RAINS, IT RAINS —
PENNIES FROM HEAVEN.

OTHERS. *(Layering in.)*

DON'T YOU KNOW EACH CLOUD CONTAINS
PENNIES FROM HEAVEN?

(Woman 4 joins the rest.)

ALL.

YOU'LL FIND YOUR FORTUNE FALLING
ALL OVER TOWN
BE SURE THAT YOUR UMBRELLA
IS UPSIDE DOWN.

TRADE THEM FOR A PACKAGE OF
SUNSHINE AND FLOWERS.
IF YOU WANT THE THINGS YOU LOVE,
YOU MUST HAVE SHOWERS.

SO WHEN YOU HEAR IT THUNDER
DON'T RUN UNDER A TREE,
THERE'LL BE PENNIES FROM HEAVEN —

PENNIES FROM HEAVEN —
PENNIES FROM HEAVEN —

FOR YOU AND ME!

(A drizzle of glistening copper pennies falls lightly from the sky as we ...)

FADE OUT

(Bows. The Band kicks in to "SWINGING ON A STAR" as the lights come up and the cast take their bows.)

ALL.

WOULD YOU LIKE TO SWING ON A STAR?
CARRY MOONBEAMS HOME IN A JAR?
AND BE BETTER OFF THAN YOU ARE?
YOU COULD BE SWINGIN' ON A STAR.

AND ALL THE MONKEYS AREN'T IN THE ZOO.
EV'RY SINGLE DAY YOU MEET QUITE A FEW.
SO, YOU SEE IT'S ALL UP TO YOU.
YOU COULD BE SWINGIN' ON A STAR!

(From above, three huge swings fly in, hanging from stars. The cast sits on the swings and as they sing — of course — they swing on a star!)

WOULD YOU LIKE TO SWING ON A STAR?
CARRY MOONBEAMS HOME IN A JAR?
AND BE BETTER OFF THAN YOU ARE?
YOU COULD BE SWINGIN' ON A STAR.

YOU CAN GO VERY FAR!
YOU CAN GO VERY FAR!
YOU CAN GO VERY FAR!

YOU COULD BE SWINGIN'-
SWINGIN' —
SWINGIN' —
SWINGIN' —

(A picture of Johnny Burke is projected onto a star high above them.)

— ON A STAR!

END OF SHOW

AUTHOR'S NOTE

Re: The transition into the USO show.

If you are unable to acquire the rights to the real voices of Walter Winchell, Edward R. Murrow, etc. but don't want to have the actors imitate them, you might try the following:

In the darkness the large Hit Parade clock hanging in the air lights up. The hands of the clock move faster and faster as years are superimposed on its face: 1936 ... 1938 ... 1941.... Interspersed by static, we hear audio snippets of various radio programs, as if someone is changing stations through time. Programs like "The Ted Mack Amateur Hour," Groucho's "You Bet Your Life," etc. Finally, we hear the tinny strains of a swing band and the Announcer's Voice.

ANNOUNCER. *(V.O.)* And now, ladies and gentlemen, coming to you live from our Allied Headquarters in the Pacific Islands — it's a USO All Star Special!

The clock has stopped at 1944 and the swing band on the radio becomes our band live on stage as the lights come up on the USO show.

If you are unable to use projections:

After the Radio Segment blackout, lights come up on the Announcer standing at his microphone in a dim pin spot. Slowly, with each broadcast, he flips the pages of his radio script so that the audience can see the years engraved on the back of each page: 1936 ... 1938 ... etc. Finally, over the tinny strains of a swing band, he announces:

ANNOUNCER. And now, ladies and gentlemen, coming to you live from our Allied Headquarters in the Pacific Islands — it's a USO All Star Special!

He exits as the lights come up to reveal the USO show.

* * *

The ROAD TO section can easily be performed without the use of the movie screen:

The lights come up on the Paramount Sound Stage — a beehive of activity. Musicians warm up in the back. An electrician in "Paramount Studios" coveralls stands on a ladder, focusing a light. Prop and wardrobe personnel mill around. An authoritative Voice cuts through the din.

DIRECTOR. *(V.O.)* All right, quiet on the set! *(All scurry off.)* Slate it, please. *(The "Slater" runs on with his chalk board.)*
SLATER. Bing, Bob and Dorothy. "Road To Morocco." Take One! *(He clacks the board and runs off.)*
DIRECTOR. *(V.O.)* Action! *(Music in as the lights change and Bing and Bob enter on the camel, singing "ROAD TO MOROCCO.")*

If you are using the movie screen, but are unable to acquire the rights to Paramount's signature logo of "The End," any "The End" logo will do. Or you can simply end the segment with Bing, Bob and Dorothy singing "We're Morocco Bound."

* * *

The following can be used for the Transition into the SUPPER CLUB (if it isn't possible to use the Stars' Voices).

A shimmering crystal curtain flies in. Man 3, dressed in a tux, enters through the curtain. A piano plays lightly in the background.

MAN 3. *(Quoting.)*
"Who can say what love is?
Does it start in the mind or the heart?
When I hear discussions on what love is
Everybody speaks a different part.

Love is funny or it's sad,
Or it's quiet or it's mad.
It's a good thing or it's bad,
But Beautiful."

(Smiles.) Poetry, isn't it? That's the beginning of *"BUT BEAUTIFUL,"* one of Johnny Burke's most haunting lyrics. You know, Johnny had a nickname. It started when he was a kid, earning extra bread by playing the piano and singing in low-down Speakeasies in Chicago. Johnny would occasionally toss in one of his own compositions, not thinking anyone would notice. Well, one day he's walking down the street and he sees two guys who frequented the club coming toward him. These guys were known for beating people up just for the hell of it. It was too late to cross the street. Johnny took a breath, kept his eyes down, and hoped for the best. Sure enough, as they passed, one of the guys went to grab Johnny, but the other guy stopped him, saying, "Leave him alone — That's The Poet." And that's how Johnny learned of his nickname. *(An introduction.)* And now, Ladies and Gentlemen, the timeless songs of The Poet — Johnny Burke. *(Man 3 exits as the crystal curtain flies out to reveal the Starlight Supper Club.)*

PROPERTY LIST

STAGE LEFT

Easel with Cha-Cha sign
2 coats
5 coat check stubs
Ashtray
Champagne bottle
Clarinet
Glass stuffed with dollar bills
Hand fan
Paper money
Peyton Place novel
Snow pouch with snow
Square box of candy
2 waiter's rags
Apple tray
USO ammunition case
Crate filled with Coke bottles
Shopping bag with handles
Radio mic with apple
Radio chairs pallet
3 radio chairs
3 3-page radio scripts
Ballroom stool with back
Ballroom stool without back
Banana tree
Burlap sack
Camel
Carpeted step
Ladder with water spritzer
2 "Supper Club" band music stand covers
Rocking horse
Junk cart with 5 signs
Dock unit
Penny
Pipe
Tobacco pouch

STAGE RIGHT

2 tree stumps
Canoe
White parasol
Dr. Rhythm music note chair
Black umbrella with penny
Street lamp pallet with trash can and 2 crates
Wine glass
10 plain glasses
2 black waiter's trays
2 4-page radio scripts
3 wooden coat hangers with 3 coat check stubs
Blue flower bouquet
Gold wedding bouquet
Heart-shaped box
Red flower bouquet
Black purse with:
    compact, cigarette case, cigarettes, lighter, and 3-$1.00 bills
2 canoe oars
Rags and pots bundle
2 radio mics with apples
USO mic
Easel with photo sign
Radio chair pallet
3 radio chairs
Car with:
    2 wipers, black umbrella, sun reflector and 3 pairs of sunglasses
USO crate unit
Lei
Gun case with trumpet inside
Tapestry
4-page radio script
Pistol
Binaca mouthwash
Flask

ONSTAGE

Glass of water on coaster
2 USO band music stand facades—rolled up
2 "Radio Show" band music stand covers
2 Speakeasy band music stand covers
Tablecloths
Table lamps
Lei rigged to drop